Wha[illegible] ook

A cogen[illegible] ded clarity for th[illegible] Anglican Commu[illegible] nt church history as our patient teacher and Scripture as our unwearied guide. This book is a timely resource.

Jon Tuckwell. Vicar, Christ Church Cockfosters

This pastoral, historical, and biblical call to contend for the truth from within the Church of England deserves to be heard. It is a call to remain, but not at any cost.

Ed Moll. Senior Minister, St George's Church Wembdon

If you are wondering about how close to stay to the Church of England, how far to run from it, how awkward to be in it, or how positive to be towards it, you will find here deep biblical wisdom with lessons from our history to help and guide us all.

Paul Darlington. Vicar of Holy Trinity Oswestry

These pieces provide useful reading for all—lay and ordained—who find themselves within the Church of England and are wondering how things might develop, and how they themselves should be making decisions. They remind us that God is in sovereign control and therefore encourage us that he is able to bring glory to his Son in any circumstance, even when an influential denomination looks as if it is succumbing to apostasy. This book will be a useful resource for both pessimists and optimists.

Debbie Buggs. Lay Member of General Synod, London

The authors of this book build up a positive picture of confident evangelical involvement in the Church of England which is humble and self aware before the Lord, and conscious of the dangers both of passive compromise and of doing something just for the sake of being seen to do something. Uncompromising in their convictions without being combative, and piercing in their critique without being partisan, they draw on deep roots in scripture, theology, and history to present a clear call to persistent faithfulness and trust in our sovereign God. I have found it very helpful and will recommend it gladly.

Dave Walker. Vicar of Christ Church North Finchley and Lecturer in Anglican Ministry at Oak Hill College, London

Gospel Flourishing in a Time of Confusion

Wisdom from the Bible and church history for Anglican Evangelicals

Edited by LEE GATISS

Contributors

Rod Thomas, Wallace Benn, James Hughes

Rob Munro, and Lee Gatiss

Gospel Flourishing in a Time of Confusion
Wisdom from the Bible and church history for Anglican Evangelicals

Published for Church Society by Lost Coin Books
email: lostcoinbooks@gmail.com
web: www.lostcoinbooks.com
Church Society
Ground Floor, Centre Block
Hille Business Estate, 132 St Albans Road
Watford WD24 4AE, UK
Tel +44 (0)1923 255410
www.churchsociety.org
admin@churchsociety.org

ISBN: 9781999327019

Printed in the UK

Contents

Contents

Preface

The following chapters began life as papers given at a Study Day organised by the Fellowship of Word and Spirit, and at the annual Church Society conference, both in May 2018.

They address some of the key questions facing Anglican Evangelicals at this moment of confusion and uncertainty in the life of the Church. Should we stay in the Church of England, and make use of the many gospel opportunities it affords? Or should we leave for pastures new, since things within the established church have become so difficult? What does it mean to be a "righteous remnant" in an apostate church, when everyone seems to be doing "what is right in their own eyes"? And are there lessons we can learn from how our forefathers handled these sorts of questions, not just in recent times but in the very earliest days of the church?

Above all, what we as evangelicals committed to the Church of England really want is for the gospel of Jesus to flourish and spread in our nation. We want to "proclaim afresh in this generation" the "inheritance of faith" which we have received, because it is such good news for all. This book is offered as a resource to help us as we think through together how best to make that happen in our day and age. May it bring wisdom and insight as we face the future.

For the glory of God and the good of England!

Revd Dr Lee Gatiss
Cambridge, Epiphany 2018

Chapter 1

Flourishing in the Church of England

Rod Thomas

How might evangelicals hope to flourish in the Church of England today? The Bible contains various pointers to what it looks like both for individuals and churches to flourish.

For the individual, Psalm 1 presents us with two ways to live. We can either 'walk', 'stand', and 'sit' sinfully, or we can delight in the law of the Lord. The one who does the latter is rooted in a life-giving place, fed by fresh water, and is healthy and fruitful.

For churches, few passages are lovelier than Ephesians 4:11–16. There, the church is pictured as growing into maturity, not being tossed to and fro by every wind of doctrine but, with members speaking the truth to each other in love, growing up into Christ.

The biblical picture of flourishing is therefore about being fruitful and growing in holiness as we take the word of God seriously. As we do that, it is clear from both texts that our flourishing will also be accompanied by those engaged in doing the opposite. So the question is, how does the Church of England enable us, in our individual and congregational lives, to flourish in this way?

Enabling flourishing

There are at least five ways in which the Church of England enables evangelicals to flourish:

1. By grounding us in clear, biblical doctrine

Canon A5 says 'The doctrine of the Church is grounded in the Holy Scriptures...' The Church of England officially supports the idea of flourishing based on God's word.

2. By helping us with governance

In any group of people, disagreements will arise and those in leadership positions may be tempted to abuse their power. We remain 'fallen' creatures. Within the Church of England, there is therefore a very helpful system of checks and balances between the respective rights and duties of PCCs, incumbents, bishops and synods.

3. By providing scope for outreach

If you want to reach the nation for Christ then it's good if you have places of worship in every community. A quick look at the statistics shows what an advantageous position the Church of England is in: with over 16,000 places of worship it has, for example, almost eight times as many churches as those in the Baptist Union of England and Wales. In addition, a quarter of all primary schools are Church of England aided or controlled.

4. By encouraging inclusivity

The Church of England sees itself as a National Church rather than a denomination. It wants involvement in community life and vice versa. That sort of outlook makes evangelistic opportunities.

5. With nationally-backed initiatives

A great example of this is the way both Archbishops encourage us to pray that friends and neighbours will meet Christ, in the global 'Thy Kingdom Come' programme which precedes each Whit Sunday. The renewed emphasis on discipleship and church planting is also very supportive.

It goes without saying that each of these good things can also take questionable turns. Doctrine can be undermined by the way in which practice is developed within particular parishes, deaneries, and even cathedrals. The balance that is achieved through our structures of governance can be subtly changed by moves towards diocesan centralisation, or understandable attempts to get parishes to pool resources. Our scope for outreach can be used for spreading revisionist as well as biblical teaching. Our inclusivity can often include too much of the world. Finally, some of the initiatives currently underway can be as much a cause of concern as a positive opportunity.

The preparation of new House of Bishops' teaching resources on marriage, sexuality, and gender (entitled *Living in Love and Faith*, due in 2020) provides a great opportunity for the church to tackle the secular mindset on issues of gender and sexuality. But, given the huge pressures on the church to change its existing doctrine and liturgy, there is great concern over the possibility that following their production, proposals will be made that lead us more in the direction the Episcopal Church in the USA has taken than into distinctive biblical witness.

Encouragements for parish congregations

Where then do these various pressures inside and outside the Church of England leave us? It seems to me that the key issue is not so much the effectiveness of the Church of England as a whole, but rather how far individual congregations are able to engage in evangelism and receive teaching from the word of God.

Much therefore depends on our ecclesiology. Within evangelicalism, the local church has always been seen as the primary unit. The issue facing us, therefore, is can our congregations—and individuals within them—flourish within the Church of England? If, in due course, a decision were to be taken to alter our doctrine on marriage and sexuality, then it would be very difficult for congregations to continue to witness with integrity if the formal doctrinal position were to be at odds with what they sought to teach.

Similarly, if our liturgy were to be changed in order to accommodate secular understandings of gender or sexuality, that too would undermine our integrity. The liturgies of the Church express its doctrine. However, despite the ways some seek to change church doctrine by pressing what is permissible to the limit, the fact remains that the current doctrine and liturgy of the Church is entirely orthodox. This means we can continue to operate with integrity and there is much to encourage parish congregations as they do so.

Clergy are free to preach without fear that they might face disciplinary measures as a result; there are good standards of housing and care for clergy; there are clear mechanisms for supporting church planting through Bishops' Mission Orders—which admittedly work more easily in some dioceses than others; conservative evangelicals continue to be funded for places at training colleges and on courses; parishes are encouraged to pursue Mission Action Plans; many schools (not just Church of England schools) welcome local church involvement in assemblies and after-school clubs; and my own role as Bishop of Maidstone is genuinely welcomed in a large number of dioceses as they seek to make a reality out of "mutual flourishing" on the issue of men's and women's ministry.

Three priorities for evangelicals

In the light of this, perhaps I could conclude by identifying three priorities for evangelicals in the Church of England if we are to flourish in the future. First, we need to encourage one another, by involvement in Church Society, by active participation in local groups (often named ReNew groups), and by helping those who are struggling with practical support.

Secondly, we must prepare now for the elections to General Synod in 2020. It is likely to be this Synod which will have to vote in the key areas of liturgy and doctrine. We particularly need lay members of Deanery Synods to stand for election so that, even if we are a minority in the House of Laity, our numbers are sufficient to prevent change in these key areas.

Thirdly, we must engage with renewed effort and enthusiasm in multiplying congregations—revitalising, planting and encouraging curates to go to the less popular places—so that the gospel spreads, individuals grow in holiness, and God is honoured by more people feeding from his word.

Rt Revd Rod Thomas *is the Bishop of Maidstone, and President of Church Society.*

Chapter 2

A Season for Secession?

Wallace Benn

When J. I. Packer and others walked out of a synod in Vancouver in June 2002, it was yet another signal of a major crisis in the Anglican Communion that has taken a bit longer to impact the Church of England. But that crisis is now upon us, and it is imperative that we think properly and theologically about how, and in what way, we should respond to our church's drift away from apostolic teaching.

Packer explained the reason for their departure in a very helpful and succinct way. The gospel, he explained, is summed up in Mark's account of the early preaching of Jesus: "The time is fulfilled, and the kingdom of God is at hand; repent and believe in the gospel" (Mark 1:15). The apostles are clear about what needs to be repented of, and this is explained in 1 Corinthians 6:9-11 in a powerful passage about the life transforming change the gospel can bring about:

> *Or do you not know that the unrighteous will not inherit the kingdom of God? Do not be deceived: neither the sexually immoral, nor idolaters, nor adulterers, nor men who practice homosexuality, nor thieves, nor the greedy, nor drunkards, nor revilers, nor swindlers will inherit the kingdom of God. And such were some of you. But you were washed, you were sanctified, you were justified in the name of the Lord Jesus Christ and by the Spirit of our God.*

If we change what the apostles call us to repent of, we have changed the gospel that Jesus preached and which the apostles bore witness to. This passage makes clear this is a first order salvation issue which affects our eternal destiny. Nothing could be more serious.

We might wish it were different but the current presenting problem facing the church is the question of homosexual practice, which is mentioned in the list above as one thing needing to be repented of. The real issue is by what authority the church lives. Is it simply going to cave in to modern political correctness and pressure, or is it determined to live by the authority of 'God's Word written', and be faithful to apostolic preaching and lifestyle?

The omens have not been good. The Pilling report, with its lack of engagement with and confidence in the Scriptures to settle the issue, is a report which has muddied the waters for the discussions which have followed. While the battle is not yet lost, there is an unhelpful and dangerous ambivalence in what the church appears to believe and practice. This could be summed up by the Archbishop of Canterbury's recent unwillingness to respond to a journalist's question about whether homosexual practice was a sin or not.

On the one hand we have been clear that heterosexual marriage between one man and one woman is what the church believes marriage to be, while on the other seeming to approve of other relationships seeking to mirror marriage as legitimate places for the expression of sexual intimacy. Even the odd bishop advocates the latter. Fudge reigns!

Given that there is still a battle to be fought for the soul of the church we love, and we must not cave in too easily by acquiescence or departure, what theological principles should guide us as to when to stay and fight or when to go?

The marks of a faithful church

The Reformers are a great help to us in this. They saw that (as Gordon Spykman puts it), "a church's existence is never self-justifying. Every church which elevates itself above the judgment of God's Word thereby forfeits its status as a true church of Christ. With an appeal to Scripture the Reformers therefore introduced a new set of criteria by which to weigh the orthodoxy and orthopraxy of a church."[1] They had to help people decide how to recognise a true

---

1 Gordon J. Spykman, *Reformational Theology: A New Paradigm for Doing Dogmatics* (Grand Rapids: Eerdmans, 1992), 441.

church from a false one in the middle of difficult and dangerous times. They were driven by two concerns. One was the danger of schism, of which they believed they were falsely accused. The other was their overriding concern to be faithful to the gospel of grace, which Luther saw as "the article of a standing or a falling church", and the apostolic witness in the Scriptures to that which was "the power of God unto salvation" (Romans 1:16).

Thomas Cranmer recognising that a church can have its "lampstand" removed (Revelation 2:5) followed Bullinger and Calvin in recognising two marks of a faithful church. Calvin expresses it clearly: "Wherever we see the Word of God sincerely preached and heard, wherever we see the sacraments administered according to the institution of Christ, there we cannot have any doubt that the Church of God has some existence, since his promise cannot fail, 'Where two or three are gathered together in my name, there am I in the midst of them.'"[2] These marks were simply the practical outworking of the older description of the church as "the one, holy, catholic and apostolic church." Under the influence of Martin Bucer, some English Reformers saw a third mark—that of godly discipline. This was seen as the safeguarding of the first two marks which centre around the apostolic faith and gospel. Ridley, bearing in mind the Christian graces which the church should display affirmed *four* marks of the church (interestingly followed in our day by John Frame in his *Systematic Theology*). Ridley says,

> *The marks whereby this church is known unto me in this dark world, and in the midst of this crooked and forward generation, are these: The sincere preaching of God's word; the due administration of the sacraments; charity; and faithful observing of ecclesiastical discipline according to the word of God....by God's grace I will live and die the child of this church.*"[3]

It is clear, I think, that Cranmer did not disagree with Bucer (or even Ridley). But Cranmer knowing that any church discipline will be exercised around the Lord's table at Holy Communion places the need for that there in the directions (rubrics) before Communion, but he also implies this in Article 19

2 *Institutes*, 4.1.9 (Beveridge translation), quoting Matthew 18:20.

3 Henry Christmas (ed.), *The Works of Bishop Ridley* (Cambridge: Cambridge University Press, 1841), 123.

when he mentions the "due" administration of the sacraments. The context of this discipline is amongst those who are "in love and charity with their neighbours."

The English Reformers departure from the Church of Rome was for the sake of gospel truth. Listen to Bishop Jewel:

> *It is doubtless an odious matter for one to leave the fellowship whereunto he hath been accustomed... Neither had we departed therefrom, but of very necessity, and much against our wills... It is true: we have departed from them, and, for so doing we both give thanks to Almighty God, and greatly rejoice in our own behalf. But yet for all this, from the primitive church, from the apostles, and from Christ we have not departed... If we be schismatics because we have left them, by what name shall they be called themselves, which have forsaken the Greeks, from which they first received their faith, forsaken the primitive church, forsaken Christ himself, and the apostles, even as children should forsake their parents?* [4]

Listen again to Packer:

> *The Church becomes visible and identifiable, not by flaunting some historical pedigree of ministerial succession, but by professing and proclaiming the apostolic Gospel by word and sacrament. On this basis the Reformers held, first, that their separation from Rome was no sin since Rome had effectively unchurched herself by corrupting the Gospel; second, their separation was no breach of the Church's unity, since neither papal government and order, nor any other particular form, was essential to that unity; third, that by recovering their own church-character through their renewed confession of the Gospel the Reformed churches had actually recovered unity, and were now waiting for Rome itself to join their new-found fellowship. The distinction was thus, in the second place, the basis for a defence of the Reformation as a renewal rather than a disruption of the Church.*[5]

---

4 John Ayre (ed.), *The Works of John Jewel: Volume 4* (Cambridge University Press, 1850), 709, 871, 882.

5 J. I. Packer, "The Doctrine and Expression of Christian Unity" in *Serving the People of God: Collected Shorter Writings of J. I. Packer. Volume 2* (Paternoster 1998), 39.

Luther was very clear that separation is necessitated by two things, both of which spring from a commitment to gospel truth and a consequent desire for the purity (or holiness) of the visible church in major doctrinal or ethical matters. The first is freedom to preach the gospel unhindered, and the second is that the church must not officially proclaim or decree something contrary to the apostolic gospel. A word also from Calvin:

> *We are not on account of every minute difference to abandon a church, provided it retain sound and unimpaired that doctrine in which the safety of piety consists,*[6] *and keep the use of the sacraments instituted by the Lord. Meanwhile, if we strive to reform what is offensive, we act in the discharge of duty.*[7]

While very concerned that godly discipline be seen in the church, Calvin also advises: "Our indulgence ought to extend much farther in tolerating imperfection of conduct."[8] It is very clear then that faithfulness to the apostolic gospel and the Saviour himself requires us to be vigilant that the church remains "a pillar and buttress of the truth"(1 Timothy 3:15), which neither erodes nor undermines that very necessary faithfulness.

Conclusion

How do we apply these principles to our situation today? It is clear that we must not run away easily but fight for the health of the church knowing that it is false doctrine and ethics that cause fracture and dislocation in the church. As Jude 18-19 says, "In the last time there will be scoffers, following their own ungodly passions. It is these who cause divisions." But equally in a Reformed church, where the Reformers sought to put loyalty to gospel truth first at great cost to themselves, it is unconscionable to say we will never leave, whatever happens! Listen to an Archbishop of York in Elizabeth I's time (Sandys): "For unity in religion not grounded upon Christ and his gospel is not concord, but conspiracy."[9] Or listen further to Jewel:

6 The French says, "the fundamental doctrine of our salvation".

7 *Institutes*, 4.1.12 (Beveridge translation).

8 *Institutes*, 4.1.13.

9 John Ayre (ed.), *The Sermons of Edwin Sandys* (Cambridge University Press, 1841), 95.

> *Of a truth, unity and concord doth best become religion, yet is not unity the sure and certain mark whereby to know the church of God. For there was the greatest unity that might be amongst them that worshipped the golden calf and among them which with one voice jointly cried against our Saviour Jesus Christ, 'Crucify him!'* [10]

In the current situation we will doubtless find that there are those who wish to move too fast in departure from the church and those who are afraid of the possible church dividing consequences of standing up for first order gospel truth. Luther found this in Karlstadt on the one hand and Melanchthon on the other when he returned from being away for a year in the castle for protection. We must exercise careful, prayerful, loving but brave patience with one another. Precipitate action unilaterally taken must be studiously avoided, as must 'empire building', but we must be clear with the authorities that if the Church of England were to officially depart from fundamental apostolic gospel truth (by synod declaration or in her liturgy which teaches what we believe), or hinder our preaching of it, or seriously fail to discipline departure from it, as it seems in danger of doing, there will be sad but necessary consequences.

Those who wish to remain loyal to their Lord and the truths of Holy Scripture must insist that unless there is adequate provision for them in an orthodox province, they will be forced to divide. At that point it is not we who are leaving the Church of God, but our denominational church which is choosing to depart from its essential apostolic and biblical foundations (Ephesians 2:20-21). Dr. Martin Davie in his excellent paper published by CEEC entitled 'Guarding the Deposit: Apostolic Truth for an Apostolic Church' has shown us the way forward, as has the most recent statement from CEEC ('Gospel, Church and Marriage—Preserving Apostolic Faith & Life') which has declared remarkable evangelical agreement on the seriousness of the situation and the church dividing nature of the issues we are facing.[11]

In the event of the above happening, careful consideration must be given

---

10 John Ayre (ed.), *The Works of John Jewel: Volume 1* (Cambridge University Press, 1845), 620.

11 See ceec.info for more details.

to issues of structure and Anglican polity, which evangelicals are not good at. In the meantime, evangelical bishops must in an episcopal church take a lead in speaking out. With a few very honourable exceptions, they have apparently remained too passive and pliable. Indeed, the whole Keele experiment of evangelicals seeking to play our part in the life and structures of the church in order to reform it is now hanging in the balance. Will the evangelical bishops individually and as a group speak up or not? If not, how are they serving the gospel cause? The best outcome would be for the church to wake up and repent, but if not, for some internal solution in the Church of England to be worked out (an orthodox province is the only really possible "internal" solution, which gives distinction and distance).

But we ought to be encouraged that the vast majority of Anglicans worldwide are on our side, and GAFCON, which expresses that fundamental gospel unity around Canon A5 and the Jerusalem Statement and Declaration, is always there to help. There is thankfully another way of being an Anglican if absolutely necessary!

But we should not be pessimistic when God is still on the throne! There are still plenty of signs of life and encouragement in the Church of England, even if the storm clouds are gathering. We need to pray and fight wisely, bravely, and well for scriptural faith and practice, knowing that is in the best interests for the health of the church and the glory of her Lord. Remember the words of the apostle John: "He who is in you is greater than he who is in the world" (1 John 4:4). But we must also be realistic and think through properly what action may be necessary in the coming days. May God have mercy on us, yet again, and revive, renew and restore his church! May we again be seen to be a gospel church, living under the authority of the Word of God.

Two more practical issues need to be mentioned:

1. Train your congregation

Back in the 1960s when the Cambridge preacher Herbert Carson left the Church of England, the great Alan Stibbs from Oak Hill asked the question of him, "What about the flock you are leaving? They will suffer!" Those of us who have presbyteral oversight of congregations must train and inform them of the issues, seek to keep them praying and contending for the truth in the structures without giving up or panicking, stay with them where possible, and only move together in brave action if it proves absolutely necessary. Please God that will yet prove unnecessary! However, we need to be willing to step up with courage to do whatever needs to be done to be faithful in our witness to the gospel of Jesus Christ and the apostolic faith.

2. Understand priorities

Our young people when going to University and looking for a church to belong to often show the same instincts as the Reformers. They look for a church that preaches the gospel and teaches the Bible knowing that it is there they will be fed, and they shy away from an over sacramentalised or liberal version of the church. It is a pity that sometimes they pass an Anglican church which is displaying the two essential marks of a faithful church for a "free church" that does the same but is more appealing because of its music or "style" of worship. But their basic understanding of gospel loyalty is surely right. The true church of Christ is seen by its faithfulness to the Gospel and the Holy Scriptures, not by what denominational title it has on its noticeboard!

Let us then prayerfully and faithfully "contend for the faith that was once for all delivered to the saints" (Jude 3).

Rt Revd Wallace Benn *is a former Bishop of Lewes.*

Chapter 3

Everyone was doing what was right in their own eyes

A Reflection on Judges 17-21

James Hughes

The purpose of this chapter is to explore how the final five chapters of Judges might help us understand our present situation in the Church of England. If that feels a bit of a stretch, the link we are exploring here is between the repeated refrain, "In those days there was no king in Israel. Everyone did what was right in his own eyes,"[1] and variations on it,[2] and where we find ourselves in the Church of England. Hopefully by the end you'll be persuaded of the relevance of Judges to today.

Obviously in a chapter of this length, dealing with about 150 verses of the Old Testament, there is not a great deal of time for much detailed exegetical discussion of every point; I will assume some things that might on another occasion need to be argued, and I will assume a level of familiarity amongst the readers of the basic narrative of Judges 17-21. That might cause you to

---

1 Judges 17:6.

2 Judges 18:1, "In those days there was no king in Israel." Judges 19:1, "In those days, when there was no king in Israel." Judges 21:25, "In those days there was no king in Israel. Everyone did what was right in his own eyes." See Daniel I. Block, *Judges, Ruth* (B & H, 1999) for how this formula operates in this section of the book.

have occasion to read it before proceeding any further, and I would commend that course of action to you.

Let me begin with one generalised but I think unquestionable statement: during the period of the Judges, leadership is a problem, and whatever else the book is about, it is about that. As we come to the closing chapters of the book, we are dealing with the issue of leadership, which is always an issue for the sheep as much as it is for the (under-)shepherds.

I have one observation to make on these chapters, and three temptations in the current situation for us to consider.

An observation: doing what was right

There is debate about how we read "in those days everyone did what was right in their own eyes." Block argues that the phrase can be taken as a variation on the phrase we find so often earlier in the book, where the people did evil in the eyes of the Lord.[3] And certainly the general conduct of God's people in Judges 17-21 is evil. Yet, I think there is more to it than that. I don't think we should read this phrase as simply "they pleased themselves." Rather, we should read it as "they sought to please God in their own way."

They were deluded, they were misguided, and so often their thinking was warped by self-interest and the surrounding culture. Their conduct was often shocking, disturbing and to this day these chapters make uncomfortable reading. And yet, these were people who, in their own way, and according to their own self-understanding, were seeking to please the Lord. The fact that their behaviour is by turns laughable and terrifying does not alter this. Let me illustrate this from Judges 17:1-6, and then say why I think it is very important to us.

In Judges 17 we meet Micah an Ephraimite, who has stolen some money from his mother. He restores it and she is grateful, and I'm sure that as we're reading this we're supposed to start thinking—what? How can this be? Where is this story going? And then we read this:

---

3 Block, *Judges*, 475-6.

> *And he restored the 1,100 pieces of silver to his mother. And his mother said, 'I dedicate the silver to the* Lord *from my hand for my son, to make a carved image and a metal image. Now therefore I will restore it to you.' So when he restored the money to his mother, his mother took 200 pieces of silver and gave it to the silversmith, who made it into a carved image and a metal image. And it was in the house of Micah"* (Judges 17:3-4).

Notice a number of things. Notice what is out of kilter here. Notice the construction of an idol. Notice that she dedicates the silver and only uses 200 of 1000 pieces of silver. Notice that she gives it to her son, and not the priest at Shiloh where the ark was. But notice the intent: I dedicate the silver to the Lord, to YHWH, to the covenant Lord, not just any old god. We might say, for want of a better word, that this is bonkers, *but she means well*. She intends to honour God.

And the plot thickens: "And the man Micah had a shrine, and he made an ephod and household gods, and ordained one of his sons, who became his priest" (Judges 17:5). Again the narrative calls us to say—What? Now we're really going for it aren't we? We have a shrine, and an ephod and Micah has installed one of his own sons as priest, despite the family being from the tribe of Ephraim not Levi. (Until, as we read in the rest of Judges 17, Micah upgrades to a Levite, at least temporarily.) Where did all this stuff come from? And what is Micah up to? Suddenly we are in a very different place than where we might think Israel should be. Micah is not just a thief, he is also an organised idolater. So here comes the punchline: "In those days there was no king in Israel. Everyone did what was right in his own eyes" (Judges 17:6).

See the point—everyone did what was right *as they sought to please God in their own way*. And if you are still not persuaded, see how Judges 17 ends: "Then Micah said, 'Now I know that the Lord will prosper me, because I have a Levite as priest'" (Judges 17:13). This again makes Micah look less in tune with reality than his mother. But also makes clear what he thinks is going on here. Block makes his case for Canaanization as the theme of the book of Judges: that the Israelites are not distinguished in their thinking from the people around them, because they have been absorbed into the surrounding culture, as God warned they would be, and cannot escape from their cultural conditioning.[4] Their religion might be syncretistic, combining elements of recognition of YHWH with recognition of local gods and practices borrowed from the worship of those gods, but syncretistic religion is essentially idolatry.

And the relevance of this for us? Well, we're all seeking to please God, aren't we? And we are all trying to find the right way to do that. It's one of the reasons we are reading this book! Therefore, we must be open to the possibility that *what seems like a good way of doing things to us is nevertheless not an action which honours God.* And in that, we must particularly be aware of activity which we assume to be right because it feels culturally appropriate. We need to be able to step back, to look to God's Word, that we might not be Canaanized; that is, that we might not start doing things just because that is the way they are done around here.

And so, having identified this observation, and cautioned ourselves as we begin to look at Judges 17-21 not to focus so much on what people are doing "out there" but on what is going on "over here," let us get into our temptations. I'm sure more than three temptations can be identified here, and these certainly overlap and do not neatly subdivide into the chapters quite as I present them. All the temptations are in some sense present in all the chapters. But here, I'll focus on how each one emerges from the individual chapter.

1. The temptation of conformity (Judges 19)

We start in Judges 19. We'll come back to chapter 18 when we deal with Judges 21. In chapter 19, we move into the second major subsection of Judges 17-21, and 19:1 flags that up in a couple of ways: "In those days, when there was no king in Israel, a certain Levite was sojourning in the remote parts of the hill country of Ephraim, who took to himself a concubine from Bethlehem in Judah."

First, we are reminded that there is no king in Israel. And then, having looked at the story of Micah, which then became in chapter 18 the story of the Danites, we meet another character of questionable morality whose story will ultimately have consequences for the whole of Israel. We meet another

4 Block, *Judges*, 57-59.

Levite. And this Levite has a concubine. After all, in the context of Judges, why not? Having a concubine is hardly the worst thing we read about here!

And then we read about how this concubine was unfaithful and went back to her father, in Judges 19:2. And so, the Levite goes to get her back, and ends up having to stay with his father-in-law for five days. We read this puzzling section about the hospitality of the father-in-law which seems to have some ulterior motive, and how the Levite has to drag himself, and lead his concubine away, and at this point we probably wonder why the narrator takes so long over it, Judges 19:3-9.

But finally, off they go, late in the day, and come to Jebus. It's time to stop, but they won't stop at a foreign city. They press on to Gibeah, a city of Benjaminites (Judges 19:10-14). One of the many ironies of the narrative is that they would probably have been safer in the foreign city than in Gibeah. Once in Gibeah, they go into the square of the city, because no one is ready to receive them. They are received by an old man—but something is not quite right (Judges 19:15-21). But reading this for the first time, I don't think anyone would expect the narrative to get quite as dark as it does.

Let's pick up the narrative in verse 22: "As they were making their hearts merry, behold, the men of the city, worthless fellows, surrounded the house, beating on the door. And they said to the old man, the master of the house, 'Bring out the man who came into your house, that we may know him.'" Now we know why they were alone in the square. Now we know why the old man took them in. This is what goes down in Gibeah. And of course the wording here deliberately echoes the men of another city in another time: "But before they lay down, the men of the city, the men of Sodom, both young and old, all the people to the last man, surrounded the house. And they called to Lot, 'Where are the men who came to you tonight? Bring them out to us, that we may know them.'" (Genesis 19:4-5).

From this point on, that story has to be at work in the background as we read about Gibeah. The old man obviously refuses this request: "And the man, the master of the house, went out to them and said to them, 'No, my brothers, do not act so wickedly; since this man has come into my house, do not do this vile thing'" (Judges 19:23). This story constantly discomforts us. Is this really only a breach of hospitality? Isn't there something more fundamental here than a bit of rudeness? Shouldn't the rebuke of the men be a little stronger than "Don't be rude to our guests?"

It gets worse: "Behold, here are my virgin daughter and his concubine. Let me bring them out now. Violate them and do with them what seems good to you, but against this man do not do this outrageous thing." (Judges 19:24). It is worth asking, how does that sentence get uttered? We might ask, in what moral universe does this kind of action appear to be correct, that a virgin daughter and concubine can be violated, so that the rules of hospitality are rightly observed? The sentiments expressed here are deeply objectionable, even if it were possible to reconstruct an understanding of how this might be 'culturally appropriate.'[5] This is doing what is right in one's own eyes, taken to an astonishing and shocking conclusion. We might speak here of a loss of reality, and ask how such a weird hierarchy of values has emerged. We might ask how, culturally, the people of Gibeah, including the old man, get to where they are, particularly given the positive portrayal of the old man in the story to this point.

Notice that all this is happening within this very respectable conversation about whether or not something is hospitable. We might ask whether or not something is respectable. It doesn't get any better: "But the men would not listen to him. So the man seized his concubine and made her go out to them. And they knew her and abused her all night until the morning. And as the dawn began to break, they let her go. 26 And as morning appeared, the woman came and fell down at the door of the man's house where her master was, until it was light" (Judges 19:25-26).

The concubine is dead, as verse 28 tells us. Used, abused, murdered. And yet no one here really seems to mind. There appears to have been a total loss of moral insight. Israel has quietly become worse than Sodom and Gomorrah. No one seems terribly bothered, certainly not about the fate of the concubine. The offence appears to lie elsewhere. The Levite takes her body home. And then this: "And when he entered his house, he took a knife, and taking hold

---

5 For a helpful discussion of various reactions to this verse and what follows, see Trent Butler, *Judges* (Thomas Nelson, 2009), 424-6, 429-30.

of his concubine he divided her, limb by limb, into twelve pieces, and sent her throughout all the territory of Israel. And all who saw it said, 'Such a thing has never happened or been seen from the day that the people of Israel came up out of the land of Egypt until this day; consider it, take counsel, and speak'" (Judges 19:29-30).

Again we ask, what do you mean "What shall we do?" We'll come in a minute to how respectability turns quickly to outrage, masking one's own guilt and insecurity; but surely the bigger question here is this: how did we get here?

And this is why this passage is important to us as we consider the temptation of conformity. Here in Judges 19, there seems to have been a particular cultural understanding of hospitality, which sets the narrative in motion, as the Levite and his concubine leave her father's house too late in the day due to the pressures of hospitality. Hospitality here hides some deeper issues which are simply not being dealt with. Whether it is the relationships between the Levite and his concubine and her father, or what is going on in Gibeah, or the old man's offer of his virgin daughter. Or even the ritual dismemberment of the concubine's corpse. There is a form here, a way of behaving, but the substance has long gone. If we were to pick a word in our culture to substitute for hospitality, it might be respectability. A veneer of respectability can hide a deeper malaise. In whatever way we express this, the problem is one of cultural conformity.

As we look at this temptation, the first thing we might do is to critique our own national culture, and identify the way in which it too so often demonstrates a warped sense of morality. There is plenty of scope to do that from this passage, however I want to focus on what it means for us. The question is a somewhat open one: in what ways might we (or might I) be tempted to cultural accommodation? That is, how might I act in a way which is right in my own eyes, and would be approved of by my peers, but which is ultimately just conforming to the surrounding culture? And by surrounding culture here we are not just to think of the surrounding culture of the nation; we are also to consider the cultural values of "conservative evangelicalism" within the Church of England.

Developing an awareness of how our values might become skewed here is challenging, precisely because our usual conversation partners will tend to reinforce not challenge our behaviours, if they share our culture. We can deceive ourselves, thinking that we are pursuing God's agenda, when we are really just acting to type. For example, we might consider opposition to be a sign that we are doing what God wants us to do, knowing that suffering comes to those who serve God faithfully. This is true, but we might also be opposed because what we are doing is wrong or unwise. Opposition does not always mean we are doing the right thing.

Perhaps we need to develop our ability to listen to other partners. To be able to hear voices from outside our constituency, whatever our constituency is, who will help us to reflect on our culture, that we might guard against doing things that are right in our own eyes.

2. The temptation of self-serving outrage (Judges 20)

The connections between chapter 19 and 20 are clear. The whole nation, from Dan to Beersheba, gathers at Mizpah before the Lord, to hear from the Levite a more or less accurate version of what happened. And so the plan is hatched: they will repay Gibeah of Benjamin for the outrage (verses 1-11). But the Benjaminites stand by the men of Gibeah, and so they too muster their troops—and so by the end of verse 17, we are paused on the edge of civil war.

We see a rapid move to war as a result of outraged sensibilities. It is hard to be sympathetic with Benjamin here, and we may actually feel that, for the first time in the narrative of Judges 17-21, the Israelites are doing the right thing. Verse 18 seems to confirm this: "The people of Israel arose and went up to Bethel and inquired of God, 'Who shall go up first for us to fight against the people of Benjamin?' And the LORD said, 'Judah shall go up first.'" Especially in comparison to how the book starts: "After the death of Joshua, the people of Israel inquired of the LORD, 'Who shall go up first for us against the Canaanites, to fight against them?' The LORD said, 'Judah shall go up; behold, I have given the land into his hand' (Judges 1:1-2).

This is looking promising. We are back to Judah, and we might therefore think that we are going to get some kind of restoration now, as the tribe that will supply the kings of Israel from David onwards acts. Perhaps here, after all that has gone before, there will be an *inclusio* of hope? No. Instead, 22,000 men of Israel are killed on the first day of fighting. Another 18,000 are killed the second day. Forty thousand killed overall, a tenth of the people. And after all it couldn't be a hopeful situation where holy war against God's enemies has turned into internal holy war. And so when the people come before the Lord for a third time, they are considerably chastened:

> *Then all the people of Israel, the whole army, went up and came to Bethel and wept. They sat there before the* LORD *and fasted that day until evening, and offered burnt offerings and peace offerings before the* LORD. *And the people of Israel inquired of the* LORD *(for the ark of the covenant of God was there in those days, and Phinehas the son of Eleazar, son of Aaron, ministered before it in those days), saying, 'Shall we go out once more to battle against our brothers, the people of Benjamin, or shall we cease?' And the* LORD *said, 'Go up, for tomorrow I will give them into your hand' (Judges 20:26-28).*

Do we see here genuine repentance? Is this a recognition of covenant relationship a return to the Lord? Perhaps, although the narrative of Judges so far would make us at the least skeptical about this, and the actions which follow might suggest otherwise. This time Benjamin is defeated, in part because of the false confidence that has come from previous victories. But that in itself creates a problem, because at the end of the chapter, this is the situation:

> *So all who fell that day of Benjamin were 25,000 men who drew the sword, all of them men of valor. But 600 men turned and fled toward the wilderness to the rock of Rimmon and remained at the rock of Rimmon four months. And the men of Israel turned back against the people of Benjamin and struck them with the edge of the sword, the city, men and beasts and all that they found. And all the towns that they found they set on fire (Judges 20:46-48).*

Notice the emphasis here on the destruction that Israel brings on Benjamin in verse 48, even though, as verses 46-7 make clear, they are defeated. And I think at this point we are supposed to start wondering whether this has all gone too far. Yes, Gibeah needed to be punished, and yes, Benjamin needed to be defeated to punish Gibeah, but why is Benjamin being razed as if this tribe were Canaanites subject to the ban? Has the justified outrage of the Israelites at Gibeah's crime become self-serving? Is this about justice, or is this now about revenge? What motivates the outrage of the Israelites?

At this point, I want to turn to application and to consider how this might impact us, in our thinking and our actions. As we reflect on the state of the Church of England today, there are situations where the actions of others within the church causes us to become outraged, and justifiably so. Whether this is something said that is clearly contrary to scripture (and therefore contrary to Anglican doctrine), or something done, or something permitted, it is worth asking the question: what motivates our outrage?

Let me speak personally. Some weeks I feel like cutting my ties with the wider church. Someone has usually done something genuinely problematic. But what motivates me? Is it a desire for truth and justice or something else? Might it be that we would probably save some money, and life would just be simpler without deanery and diocese to concern myself with? I could minister in comfort and security knowing my nearest Bishop was hundreds of miles away in Surrey.

And then also, given what happens to Israel in this chapter, must I not also be cautious that my outrage is merely there to cover my own character failings, or born out a desire to *do something* when faced with situations beyond my control? None of this is intended to deny the real problems and issues that we face in the church, nor is it to suggest that passivity is the right way forward. However, we would be wise to seek greater cognisance of our own motives and motivations, so as not to assume that justified outrage was a justification in and of itself.

And so we come to the final temptation.

3. The temptation of success (Judges 18 and 21)

Here we are looking at two chapters that, whilst quite different, underline the same basic issue: the temptation of success, or of pragmatism, of doing what works.

We start in chapter 18. The Danites have been unable to secure the land God has apportioned them, and so they are heading north, looking for an easier inheritance. They come to Micah and his Levite, who they recognise from back down south. They are on a (self-appointed) journey as he Lord's people so naturally: "And they said to him, 'Inquire of God, please, that we may know whether the journey on which we are setting out will succeed.' And the priest said to them, 'Go in peace. The journey on which you go is under the eye of the Lord'" (Judges 18:5-6).

The implication of the priest's words is that God is blessing the Danites, although he doesn't quite say that. There is no evidence that this is actually the case, but the forms have been observed, and so the blessing can be given and received. And so they head on and scout out the land, and it is good. The end of the spies' report: "They said, 'Arise, and let us go up against them, for we have seen the land, and behold, it is very good. And will you do nothing? Do not be slow to go, to enter in and possess the land. As soon as you go, you will come to an unsuspecting people. The land is spacious, for God has given it into your hands, a place where there is no lack of anything that is in the earth'" (Judges 18:9-10).

Don't miss the resonance with Numbers, and Joshua and Caleb. The spies were ignored then—don't ignore them now. There is another reversal: in Numbers the spies were appointed by God; here they are self-appointed. It should come as no surprise to us by this point that it is the word of man that the Danites are following. And they go, collecting Micah's Levite along the way. The Levite decides that serving a tribe is better than serving Micah, and so he goes with them, along with all the trappings: household gods, ephod and so on. Why do the Danites do this? Because they can.

Micah comes out to complain, and then: "And the people of Dan said to him, 'Do not let your voice be heard among us, lest angry fellows fall upon you, and you lose your life with the lives of your household.' Then the people of Dan went their way. And when Micah saw that they were too strong for him, he turned and went back to his home" (Judges 18:25-26). There is no attempt to justify this behaviour as godly or righteous. It is merely doable, so it is done. And so they come to the place they have chosen: "But the people of Dan took what Micah had made, and the priest who belonged to him, and they came to Laish, to a people quiet and unsuspecting, and struck them with the edge of the sword and burned the city with fire" (Judges 18:27).

It is not hard to see where the narrator's sympathies lie. "Quiet and unsuspecting", also in verse 7, describes a people who do not get what they deserve. But the city is rebuilt, and named Dan. Nothing like erasing the past to be sure of the future. And then the sting in the tail: "And the people of Dan set up the carved image for themselves, and Jonathan the son of Gershom, son of Moses, and his sons were priests to the tribe of the Danites until the day of the captivity of the land. So they set up Micah's carved image that he made, as long as the house of God was at Shiloh" (Judges 18:30-31).

Dan does two things that are apparently successful in this chapter. They take Laish, and they take Micah's idol and priest. They both work. But clearly here, these decisions work together for long-lasting negative consequences. Rather than being in the south, between Judah and Ephraim, Dan is now in the north, the first to fall to Assyria, often isolated and vulnerable, and apostate, or at least syncretistic, from the very beginning.

So we move on to chapter 21, for a different narrative but with the same implications for us: "Now the men of Israel had sworn at Mizpah, 'No one of us shall give his daughter in marriage to Benjamin' (Judges 21:1). Not for the first time in Judges, the Israelites find themselves on the wrong end of a hasty vow. You might think they would have learned the lesson of Jephthah, but then Judges is a book all about lessons not being learned. There is a problem, because Benjamin has been all but wiped out. Only 600 men are left, after the orgy of destruction at the end of chapter 20. How can they find wives for these men, when no one will give their daughters to them?

But as well as this hasty vow, they have made another, to all assemble at Mizpah, and this offers a way out: "And they said, 'What one is there of the tribes of Israel that did not come up to the Lord to Mizpah?' And behold, no one had come to the camp from Jabesh-gilead, to the assembly (Judges 21:8). So, naturally enough, they put Jabesh-gilead to the sword: "So the congregation sent 12,000 of their bravest men there and commanded them, 'Go and strike the inhabitants of Jabesh-gilead with the edge of the sword; also the women and the little ones. This is what you shall do: every male and every woman that has lain with a male you shall devote to destruction'" (Judges 21:10-11).

Notice the language of the ban here: *devote to destruction*. But this is not a command of the Lord, this is pure opportunism. Hasty vow piles upon hasty vow, until 400 virgins are brought back for the Benjaminites. The tragedy here is not just the wanton destruction of these chapters. The tragedy is also the certainty of the Israelites that they are doing the right thing, because it works. Success brings an assurance of righteousness.

However, even though the plan has worked, there is a still a problem as 200 more wives are needed for Benjamin, but still no one can give their daughter in marriage. So another scheme is hatched, to allow the Benjaminites to take wives from the festival at Shiloh, a festival which looks very like the festivals of the Canaanites. And then when they have taken wives: "And when their fathers or their brothers come to complain to us, we will say to them, 'Grant them graciously to us, because we did not take for each man of them his wife in battle, neither did you give them to them, else you would now be guilty.' And the people of Benjamin did so and took their wives, according to their number, from the dancers whom they carried off. Then they went and returned to their inheritance and rebuilt the towns and lived in them" (Judges 21:22-23).

This getting around the ban through self-serving sophistry, as well as the casual attitude to the violence done to the women of Shiloh sounds very like the old man of Gibeah. It would seem that the attitude of the men of Gibeah is actually an attitude shared by the people of Israel more widely. Notice here that the self-serving sophistry of the people of Israel leads to the oppression of the weak by the strong. This is how pragmatism often works, as it is predicated on what I or we can achieve. That achievement is so very often at the expense of others, who by their inability to resist are shown to be weak.

Again, superficially as we read the closing verses of Judges 21, and of the book of Judges, we might think that all is well that ends well. Benjamin returns, and Israel returns. It has all worked. The problem is solved. But we finish where we began: "In those days there was no king in Israel. Everyone did what was right in his own eyes" (Judges 21:25).

So we make the obvious application, I think. Success is not the same as faithfulness. Just because it works doesn't mean it was the right thing to do. And I've left this one to last, partly because it covers the last chapter, but partly because I think this is the area of temptation that most impacts on us. Let me give a few examples of where I think this might impact us.

First, a right concern for growth in numbers, whether through growing existing congregations or planting new churches doesn't make this success criteria the sole, or even the main consideration when we act. We would never wish to reduce our narrative of evangelism and discipleship to "it grew therefore it was right", but when things are apparently working is often not the time when we are most self-reflective. Therefore, because planting a church is a sign of growth, at least initially, we need to be careful to be self-reflective.

Second, I have already highlighted the implicit comparison between the spies in Judges 18 and Numbers. A particular temptation is to look to past actions that have worked well, and to seek to replicate them, even if circumstances have changed, and even if the original situation was unique. Think how the idea of the eighteenth century revival, and its attendant applications—whether that is working outside the system, the need for altar calls, not being too worried about theology and working together (the applications are myriad)—has continuing power today. The argument is deceptively straightforward: this worked then, so this is what we do now.

And then finally, it is tempting to say all's well that ends well. It doesn't matter how we get there, as long as we get there. And yet clearly it does matter. We may mean well, and we may all be trying to do what we think is the right thing to do, and we may have different views on that, and of course there is room for disagreement on tactics going forward. But at the same time, we must attempt to evaluate our actions and hold them up to God's word, to ask if we are truly being faithful, or if we are just doing what is right in our own eyes.

Revd Dr James Hughes *is the Vicar of St Alkmund, Duffield and St Paul, Little Eaton in the Diocese of Derby.*

Chapter 4

Remaining Faithful

The Significance of the Remnant in the Prophets and today

Rob Munro

The theology of "the remnant" is crucial to understanding the application of the covenant of God to his people. How does God keep a promise to save and bless his people, or indeed through them to bless all nations,[1] when they are actively rebelling against him? How does an unconditional covenant intersect with the command for faith, repentance, and obedience? And if the covenant includes blessings and curses, what are the faithful to do when, as a minority within the nation or a church, they come under the curses of the covenant? It is through the idea of the remnant that God continues to be faithful to his promises, even when bringing judgment on his people. There are always some, saved by God's grace, who remain faithful through judgment, and become the focus of the continuing covenant of God.

What I want to explore is the biblical responsibility or purpose of that remnant in relation to others who are under judgment. Are they simply *survivors*—those who still have a faith after judgment destroys the rest, called to carry on as they had before? Are they the faithful—those whose exemplary

1 Genesis 12:3 "...in you all the families of the earth shall be blessed."

faith is preserved by God so as to be a model of faithfulness to others? Are they the future—those who refocus the covenant on themselves as others are pruned away, so the covenant promises now focus on them, as the new elect, not others? So in a time of God's judgment, are the remnant called to cling on secretly, speak up awkwardly, or move away separately from others under judgment

Background

The idea of the remnant in the Old Testament, often translating the Hebrew terms *she'ar* or *she'erit*, in its simplest sense just refers to "what is left" after some event; but it comes from the same root as "leaven" in bread-making,[2] where a small lump of yeast-mixed dough from a previous batch was kept back to mix with new flour and water to make a new batch sharing the characteristics of the old.[3] In the New Testament, following the Greek translation of the Hebrew, the terms *leimma* and *hupoleimma* carry the same sense. The significance is that the portion that remains is not just "left over", it may be the foundation of the future growth; which is why, when applied to the people of God, the faithfulness of the remnant carries significance—the few who endure are to be the catalyst for the faith of a new generation.

That theme of a faithful remnant preserved to secure the future for God's people is invariably linked to the context of the judgment of God, judging the nations, or judging the ungodliness of God's people. When judging a wider group, the remnant is usually saved to vindicate God's righteousness. In the flood narrative, the single faithful family secures the future of all humanity (Genesis 9:19). When Sodom and Gomorrah are judged, God reveals to Abraham that a large enough faithful remnant would have preserved them (Genesis 18:20-33); although graciously Lot's family are still saved. Joseph understood his calling as a means of preserving God's people through the great famine: "God sent me ahead of you to preserve for you a remnant on earth and to save your lives by a great deliverance" (Genesis 45:7). The rem-

2 Galen Peterson, "The Concept of the Remnant as a Key to Understanding God's Message of Redemption" (Presented at 68th Evangelical Theological Society Nov 2016), 1.

3 See George B. Eager, "Leaven," in James Orr (ed.), *International Standard Bible Encyclopedia* (Chicago: Howard-Severance, 1915), 3:1862 on bread-making in biblical times.

nant serves as a witness to God's power to save to a world under his judgment. But even in Genesis there are indications that the way God's covenant to Abraham is to be fulfilled is through a faithful remnant. It is Jacob who inherits the promises, not Esau, despite him being a descendant of Abraham; and given Jacob's reputation,[4] this narrowing of the application of the covenant is clearly by grace not merit.

From the Exodus onward, however, the idea develops that a remnant are saved when God judges his people, when they become disobedient. Joshua and Caleb became effectively the final faithful remnant from a faithless generation under judgment, the rest of whom die during the 40 years in the wilderness (Numbers 14:1-38). They then model true faith for a new generation (Joshua 1:16). Elijah was the sole faithful prophet (1 Kings 18:22) in all Israel, although God reveals there are 7000 others as a faithful remnant too (1 Kings 19:15-18). These remnant are those who secure a continuing faithfulness among an unfaithful people.

The prophets before the Exile

It is through the prophets that the concept of remnant becomes more prominent. Before the exile of Israel to Assyria, "remnant" has a largely negative connotation for the prophet Amos. The remnant are like bits of a sheep rescued from a lion's mouth, or straggles of a massacred army (Amos 3:12, 5:3).[5] However, having prophesied the decimation of Israel, Amos contemplates that through repentance and faith," it may be that the Lord, the God of hosts, will be gracious to the remnant of Joseph." (Am 5:15). The remnant exists just to show that God hasn't been totally defeated.

Isaiah elaborates on that theme of mercy after judgment, by prophesying that after the judgment on his people through the Assyrians' victory and Israel's

4 This is anticipated in his naming. "Jacob" has connotations of deception, and his exploits included deceiving his brother to acquire the birthright (Genesis 25:31-34), deceiving his father to obtain a blessing (Genesis 27), and although deceived by Laban over his wives (Genesis 29) and his wages (Genesis 30), even his re-acquaintance with Esau seems manipulative (sending advance bribes before meeting, chapter 33).

5 Joseph Blenkinsopp, *Open the Sealed Book: Interpretations of the Book of Isaiah in Late Antiquity* (Eerdmans, 2006), 223.

exile, God would then judge the Assyrians and renew his people. Having named his son *she'ar jashub*, "a remnant will return", as a sign of God's purpose beyond judgment, Isaiah then prophesies:

> *In that day the remnant of Israel and the survivors of the house of Jacob will no more lean on him who struck them, but will lean on the LORD, the Holy One of Israel, in truth. A remnant will return, the remnant of Jacob, to the mighty God. For though your people Israel be as the sand of the sea, only a remnant of them will return. Destruction is decreed, overflowing with righteousness. For the Lord GOD of hosts will make a full end, as decreed, in the midst of all the earth (Isaiah 10:20-23).*

Significantly, the return of the remnant here is understood as their return to the Lord, not specifically a return from Assyria. Later in Isaiah's ministry, that same remnant principle is applied to the faithful in Judah who survive the siege of Assyria: "And the surviving remnant of the house of Judah shall again take root downward and bear fruit upward. For out of Jerusalem shall go a remnant, and out of Mount Zion a band of survivors. The zeal of the LORD of hosts will do this" (Isaiah 37:31-32). This remnant is an act of grace, a work of the Lord—and the distinctive faithfulness of the remnant is a response to God's grace not the cause of it! The future of God's people is secured by God graciously enabling them to survive his judgment, which renews their faith and faithfulness in him. They are survivors, but by grace they re-establish faithfulness in the future.

Isaiah realises this principle of remnant has an additional eschatological significance. In the days of the Messiah, there will be a regathering of the faithful remnant from all the nations, as significant as the Exodus.

> *"In that day the root of Jesse, who shall stand as a signal for the peoples—of him shall the nations inquire, and his resting place shall be glorious. In that day the Lord will extend his hand yet a second time to recover the remnant that remains of his people, from Assyria, from Egypt, from Pathros, from Cush, from Elam, from Shinar, from Hamath, and from the coastlands of the sea.*
>
> *He will raise a signal for the nations*
> *and will assemble the banished of Israel,*

and gather the dispersed of Judah
from the four corners of the earth....
And there will be a highway from Assyria
for the remnant that remains of his people,
as there was for Israel
when they came up from the land of Egypt (Isaiah 11:10-12, 16).

The blessing of the nations under the covenant will be revealed not by a universalism that saves them all, but by comprehensivism, a remnant of God's people will be found in every nation. A new people are formed by reuniting the remnants of God's people across the world. The survivors become the new people of God!

These themes are expanded on by Micah, who prophesies about the Messiah leading the remnant (2:12-13), those who are "lame" (4:6-7), with no strength of their own, will be gathered as God's people. But he goes on to describe the divine purpose of the remnant:

Then the remnant of Jacob shall be
in the midst of many peoples
like dew from the Lord,
like showers on the grass,
which delay not for a man
nor wait for the children of man.
And the remnant of Jacob shall be among the nations,
in the midst of many peoples,
like a lion among the beasts of the forest,
like a young lion among the flocks of sheep,
which, when it goes through, treads down
and tears in pieces, and there is none to deliver.
Your hand shall be lifted up over your adversaries,
and all your enemies shall be cut off (Micah 5:7-9).

This emphasises a twin purpose for the remnant: to bring a blessing from God to some, like dew or showers; or else to bring judgment on others, like a lion destroying its foes. The remnant will result in blessing for some, but judgment for others, or in New Testament language, at the same time the fragrance of life and death (2 Corinthians 2:15-16).

By the time of Zephaniah, after the exile of Israel, while prophesying the destruction of Judah and Jerusalem, the remnant of Judah is now promised divine protection (Zephaniah 2:7) and a reward of plunder as a result of God's judgment on other nations in due course (Zephaniah 2:9), but they will be a people humbled and purified by God (Zephaniah 3:11-13). The covenant blessings on God's people, of rescue, rest and reward, are seen to belong not to all Israel or Judah, but just to the remnant.

In all these cases, the remnant demonstrate the continuity of the covenant of God with his people. Their survival witnesses to his power and grace to save, even from his own judgment; but their renewed faithfulness witnesses to God's renewed presence and purpose for his people through them. They are trophies of grace, models of faith and visible pledges of God's covenant, the catalyst for God's future purposes. But what is emphasised is the continuity of God's people—they are not a new start, God's plan B; they are those with a renewed heart, whose faithfulness to God's Word and experience of God's blessing become the catalyst for God's covenant purposes to pass to the next generation.

But even as the pre-exilic prophets see the exile of Israel to Assyria as establishing a remnant in Judah as a warning to them to be faithful, the warnings of a final judgment are renewed. The faithful that remain are fewer and in the end the prospect of the final failure of the people of God looms as Babylon looms.

The prophets during the Exile

So it is under the ministry of Jeremiah that the principle of the remnant has a significant new development. A distinction is made between a remnant that simply remains as survivors after the exile of Jerusalem to Babylon, a national Israel, who remain under God's judgment (which also includes another remnant of them that escape to Egypt after the fall of Jerusalem, Jeremiah 42:15. 44:12-14); and a different remnant that is exiled to Babylon, who are promised God's blessing and renewal. It is this remnant that are promised blessing during exile (Jeremiah 29:5-7), a return to the land (Jeremiah 23:3,

29:1ff, 31:7), forgiveness of their sin (Jeremiah 50:20), and the ones through whom a new forgiven, heart-renewed covenant will be established (Jeremiah 31:31-34).

Two aspects of this are particularly significant: first, the faithful remnant are now defined apart from the external signs of covenant blessing, the temple and the land. There is this biblical precedent for being separated from the symbols of God's promise, if the people and its leaders become unfaithful to God—although the faithful are not willingly exiled from them. It is not the external signs that matter—but the Word of God and the presence of God—and both are to be found in exile! But second, it is significant that Jeremiah himself remains with those he knows are destined for destruction—called to suffer the consequences of their rebellion, while continuing, at great personal cost, to proclaim God's unpalatable truth to them. He stays among the reprobate people so that their continued rebellion against God's word justifies his judgment. He is called to continue to minister among those whom God is rejecting under judgment, not to escape to the place of his blessing—no wonder he is renowned for being so depressed about his calling—but even those branches being cut off from the vine, are still given God's word, with the hope that they may one day heed it and perhaps be grafted in again. It is not a remnant of faith, but there is a reminder for them of God's word of judgment—as testimony to others that it was God who allowed their destruction.

Ezekiel also proclaims the destruction of the remnant who remain in Judah after the first exile to Babylon, as a vindication of God's justice on their ongoing rebellion and sin (Ezekiel 5:10-13, 6:10-14, 7:14-16, 9:4-10, 17:21). This is powerfully brought home to him by his vision of the glory of the Lord departing the temple (Ezekiel 10:18-19). In contrast, having already had a vision of that same glory now in Babylon (Ezekiel 1), he is shown that those in exile are the ones who are now promised to be preserved by God, restored to the land and become the catalyst for spiritual renewal (11:15-20). The covenant promises are now to be fulfilled in them. Ezekiel sums this up just before his vision of a new temple:

> *Therefore thus says the Lord GOD: Now I will restore the fortunes of Jacob and have mercy on the whole house of Israel, and I will be jealous*

for my holy name. They shall forget their shame and all the treachery they have practiced against me, when they dwell securely in their land with none to make them afraid, when I have brought them back from the peoples and gathered them from their enemies' lands, and through them have vindicated my holiness in the sight of many nations. Then they shall know that I am the LORD *their God, because I sent them into exile among the nations and then assembled them into their own land. I will leave none of them remaining among the nations anymore. And I will not hide my face anymore from them, when I pour out my Spirit upon the house of Israel, declares the Lord GOD (Ezekiel 39:25-29).*

The purpose of the now Spirit-filled returning remnant is to demonstrate God's holiness and grace to the world, and renew the place of God's presence under the Messiah's rule (Ezekiel 37:21-28). And what will characterise this renewed remnant? They will willingly obey the Word of God (37:24) and know the presence of God in their midst (37:27).

So was the aftermath of exile as glorious as was hoped?

After the Exile

Given the hope for renewal at the return from exile, it is striking that the post-exilic prophets largely identify the remnant simply as survivors—those who have returned from exile, wrestling to return God's people to faithfulness. Haggai (1:12.14, 2:2) calls them to obedience and temple-building with the God's assurance, "I am with you" (1:13, 2:4). Zechariah promises by grace for the remnant to be a blessing to the nations because his presence will once again dwell in Jerusalem (Zechariah 8:3-13), but also anticipates a further future refining judgment and new remnant, this time associated with the Messiah

"Awake, O sword, against my shepherd,
against the man who stands next to me,"
declares the LORD *of hosts.*
"Strike the shepherd, and the sheep will be scattered;
I will turn my hand against the little ones.
In the whole land, declares the LORD,

two thirds shall be cut off and perish,
and one third shall be left alive.
And I will put this third into the fire,
and refine them as one refines silver,
and test them as gold is tested.
They will call upon my name,
and I will answer them.
I will say, 'They are my people';
and they will say, 'The LORD is my God'" (Zechariah 13:7-9)

Malachi also anticipates a further revealing of a remnant within the post-exilic community, where sin had crept in.

Then those who feared the LORD spoke with one another. The LORD paid attention and heard them, and a book of remembrance was written before him of those who feared the LORD and esteemed his name. "They shall be mine, says the LORD of hosts, in the day when I make up my treasured possession, and I will spare them as a man spares his son who serves him. Then once more you shall see the distinction between the righteous and the wicked, between one who serves God and one who does not serve him" (Malachi 3:16-18).

It is part of keeping covenant that God continually calls for a visible differentiation between those of his people who are faithful to his word, and those who are disobedient; but the primary mechanism for this is the preservation of the faithful through judgment, rather than their separation from the people to avoid judgment. Jesus makes the same point in the analogy of John 15: A gardener prunes a vine for fruitfulness, and it involves removing deadwood and cleansing/pruning good wood, but it leads to a fruitfulness that in turn exhibits true faithfulness (John 15:1-8). There is pain in remaining in the vine, no fruit separate from it.

So if the principle of remnant continues beyond the exile, does it still apply under the new covenant?

New Testament Reflections

At the heart of Jesus' teaching is the recognition of a distinction between those who are truly regenerate and demonstrate the fruit of the Spirit, and those who give lip-service to obedience and are unfruitful (e.g. Matthew 7:15-23... "Not everyone who says to me, 'Lord, Lord,' will enter the kingdom of heaven"). Various passages pick up that remnant theme. In Matthew 7:13-14 only the few find the small gate and narrow road that leads to life, while the many walk to destruction. In Matthew 24:40-41 at the second coming it is only a faithful remnant who remain after judgment falls.[6] Even in Revelation 11:13, only a terrified remnant glorify God after surviving a severe earthquake which judges the city who had killed the two faithful witnesses.

However it is Paul's exposition of the remnant in Romans 9-11 that has exercised most New Testament scholars' interest, not least because of his explicit links to the concept in Isaiah. Paul argues that God's promise to Israel has not failed, despite only a small number of Jews believing, because both Jews and Gentiles have been called by grace for glory (Romans 9:24); and he then cites Isaiah 10:22-23 (in 9:27) and Isaiah 1:9 (in 9:29) to establish that God's promise is still being kept when only a remnant survives. This is reinforced in Romans 11:1-6 by reference to Elijah and the 7000 faithful of his day, and the "remnant chosen by grace" (11:5). That leads him to a distinction within "Israel": "Israel failed to obtain what it was seeking. The elect obtained it, but the rest were hardened" (Romans 11:7). The significance of this is less the speculation about the future of a national Israel,[7] and more that within the church of God there will be some hardened to obedience and a remnant committed to faithfulness by grace, just as there was under the Old Covenant.[8]

---

6 Unlike some dispensational interpretations of this passage, where "being taken" implies rapture, here it is being taken as analogous to how the flood fell on the people in Noah's day.

7 This arises out of the comment in Romans 11:25-26, "a partial hardening has come upon Israel, until the fullness of the Gentiles has come in. And in this way all Israel will be saved." However, the accompanying quotation from Jeremiah 31:33-34 clarifies that the forgiveness of "Jacob" is through the forgiveness brought by the "deliverer", not via a misplaced nationalism, given that Jeremiah himself is making that point in that passage.

8 See John M. Frame, *The Doctrine of God: A Theology of Lordship* (P&R Publishing, 2002),

This principle is applied poignantly in the letters to the seven churches in Revelation. Ephesus is told to repent or be removed (Revelation 2:5); Pergamum must repent or end up fighting God (Revelation 2:16); Thyatira will see those compromising morality with "Jezebel" struck dead (Revelation 2:23); and Sardis has only a small faithful remnant left uncorrupted (Revelation 3:4). The significance is that the Lord of the churches exercises his right even to completely remove a church's lampstand for unfaithfulness. That pattern of keeping covenant through a remnant continues under the new covenant, until Judgment Day, and only then by grace will holiness and love perfectly reign in the hearts of his people.

Applications and Implications

1. Remnants remain!

They are the way God continues the covenant promises to a new generation through whatever judgment he brings on unfaithfulness in a previous one. They remain true to God's word—they obey it when others abandon it. They remain conscious of God's presence—they are holy when others are corrupt. But they remain identified with the people of God—visibly differentiated from those under judgment, they continue to stand up for God's word and ways even at great personal cost, and sometimes, like Jeremiah, knowing that their faithfulness will not change stubborn hearts—but he stood up amongst them anyway!

Question: If we aren't forced out of a church because our faithfulness gets disciplined, will we still remain faithful to God's word and holiness amongst oth-

---

322, "And in Christ, by his grace, all believers belong to the remnant (Rom.11:1-6. This remnant includes both Jews and Gentile... As not all Israelites are Israel (9:6), so not all members of the Christian church are regenerate believers. Some are elect only as the unbelieving Israelites were: historically elect, rather than eternally elect. Like Saul and Judas, they are chosen only temporarily; they can become nonelect. So the election of the visible Christian church is similar to the election of the Old Testament Israel. It is an election that temporarily includes some within its bounds who will never come to a true faith and will never have eternal life. This parallel between the church and Israel should not be surprising because the church and Israel are, contrary to dispensationalism, the same body. The tree of redemption is one, and God prunes it and grafts branches onto it, in accordance with his will."

ers who abandon that way? It was God's judgment that separated the remnant from the covenant blessings of land and temple, not their own judgment that things were too corrupt. Indeed Jeremiah stayed with the reprobates not the blessed because they still let him live among them.

2. Remnants resist!

They are marked out by their faithfulness to God's word, when it is generally neglected; and faithful to God's holiness, when it is generally corrupted. That will lead to confrontation—Elijah, Isaiah, Jeremiah all challenged the religious-political status quo by proclaiming uncomfortable truths, declaring judgment on the unfaithfulness they could see.

Question: Are we willing to actually proclaim God's judgment on unfaithfulness? Where God's word is distorted and God's holiness corrupted the remnant challenge it—by their words, proclaiming God's unpalatable truths; and by their life—living distinctively in holiness in their generation. While it is not being faithful that preserves them (grace alone does that), being faithful shapes future generations.

3. Remnants revive!

They are the way God chooses to renew his covenant promises for a future generation. Their faithfulness is not a just a witness to truth, they are the seed of new growth. So just as the remnant in Jerusalem survive the Assyrian invasion through Hezekiah's revival, or the exiles in Babylon reseed the land of promise, so God establishes foundations for future blessing through his remnant.

Question: Are we modelling sacrificial faith to future generations? Are we helping others see how to survive God's judgment and recapture a passion for God's word and holiness? Are we willing to even lose the battle of our day, knowing that we have laid faithful foundations for future generations?

4. Remnants repent!

There is no triumphalism in surviving God's judgment. There is only grief! Each time God preserves a remnant, they are characterised by repentance, by lamenting their deserving of judgment and returning to the Lord to depend on his grace to save them.

Question: Are we repenting of what we see our church doing? Or are we accommodating it somehow? Until we lament the unfaithfulness, and repent in a renewed prayerfulness, we may not be the remnant that God is creating for his future. That has to be a defining mark of any godly future. If a divide comes, who will be lamenting and repenting? What did the faithful do by the rivers of Babylon—they wept! If we dare to think of ourselves as a remnant, we need to examine ourselves to be repentant.

Conclusion

Through the remnant, God keeps his covenant. Through a remnant God may justly judge those who are unfaithful to him and yet gracious save those who remain faithful. He preserves a people for himself, even in the midst of his judgment, as testimony to his sovereignty and grace. He establishes their faithfulness as a catalyst for re-establishing his people after judgment. Ultimately he refocuses his covenant promises upon them, so that the remnant become those through whom the future blessings of his covenant will come. But they are a remnant remaining as evidence of God's faithfulness; resisting as witnesses to his truth; repenting in tears for their own generation, and reviving the next generation. It was never without cost; but always for God's glory!

Revd Dr Rob Munro *is the Rector of St Mary, Cheadle and Rural Dean in the Diocese of Chester.*

Chapter 5

Leaving and Remaining

A Brief History of Secession

Lee Gatiss

In this chapter, I want to try and give a little bit of historical perspective on the issue of secession from the Church of England. This has been the elephant in the room in many Anglican conversations over the last two decades: when are we leaving? Or to mix up all the metaphors: what will be the red line in the sand that breaks the camel's back and tips us all over the edge into secession?

In recent times, this debate has become as fraught as the debate over Europe, with Remainers and Leavers arguing over the timing and the terms of Brexit, or as we might call it in our ecclesiastical context, Chexit. And just as with Brexit, there is a variety of options for a hard Chexit or a soft Chexit.

We must be clear and acknowledge the growing anxieties which are pushing us towards a consideration of this subject:

1. We feel instinctively the displeasure of God at our society and our church. The evangelical conscience is deeply disturbed by the moral climate of the nation and the doctrinal and disciplinary chaos in the established church, such that it is not right to simply "keep our heads down in the parishes" as many of our forefathers once did (perhaps to our cost).

2. We also feel keenly the displeasure of the hierarchy, given the obsta-

cles we face within the Church of England as complementarian and conservative evangelicals. Our lack of representation amongst the bishops and senior clergy, the hindrances faced by our ordinands and curates as they try to find a place to serve, and the increasing emptiness of the rhetoric of "flourishing" are upsetting to many.

3. We sense the uselessness of the Church of England system to combat rampant secular atheism and the widespread ignorance and misrepresentation of our common faith. General Synod panders to anecdotal emotionalism, archbishops dismissively denounce those who stand firm on God's "word word word", and there seems more energy given to virtue signalling the rich, liberal provinces of the Communion than in standing shoulder to shoulder with gospel partners in the Global South.

4. Finally, the apparent direction of travel on issues of gender and sexuality gives rise to intense discomfort not just for Anglican evangelicals here but for gospel partners in other denominations and orthodox brothers and sisters around the world. We may not buy the Marxist doctrine of historical inevitability so beloved of revisionists, who say we are "on the wrong side of history" and that their final victory is assured; but the trajectory at the moment gives little cause for optimism.

I know there is a counter-narrative on all these points. The Church of England's discipline has held in some high profile cases recently. We do have Rod Thomas as Bishop of Maidstone, and some other generally orthodox bishops. Many local parish churches and parachurch ministries are standing firm, even if national institutions are wobbling or worse. And the official position of the Church of England remains the traditional one on sex and marriage. For now.

All the same, the pressure points are there, and the displeasure of God, the displeasure of the hierarchy, the frustrating impotence of the national church, and the seeming direction of travel are all reasons why secession has again become a hot topic. Something must be done. Secession is something. So perhaps we should do it?

I think that's faulty logic. Doing the wrong thing can be worse than doing nothing. What we must try to do is the right thing. But as Grayson Carter says in his study of Protestant secessions in the early nineteenth century: because of tensions in the Anglican Communion, "at no time in the history of the church have such secessions occurred as frequently, or the study of them become more relevant, as during the past decade."[1]

So how did evangelicals navigate this tension in days gone by? And is there anything we can learn from the past? I want to look at some key moments in the last 500 years to see what we can find. We will look at the Brownists of the 16th century, the ejected puritans of 1662, the Non-Jurors, and briefly at the Methodists, some nineteenth-century seceders, and a quick glance at the last century too.

So, to kick off, let me take you back to the days of the Reformation, as we consider first the Brownists.

The Brownists

In the late sixteenth and early seventeen centuries, the words puritan and nonconformist meant someone *within* the Church of England who objected to various practices. They didn't like wearing surplices or wedding rings or signing babies with the sign of the cross after baptism. But they remained within the Church of England as a force for change.

As Patrick Collinson has shown in his book on *The Elizabethan Puritan Movement*, the Puritans were a reforming movement *within* the Church of England. Although they formed something of a church within a church, with alternative networks of fellowship behind the official structures, and sometimes regarded bishops simply as civil magistrates rather than their spiritual leaders, their primary aim under Elizabeth I was not political restructuring.[2]

There were a few, however, who went so far as to advocate for separation of the truly godly from the national church. These were called separatists or Brownists, after Robert Browne (1550-1633) one of the earliest and most influential of this group. Around 1580, Browne rejected the offer of a church in Cambridge and decided to pursue "Reformation without tarrying for any", in

1 Grayson Carter, *Anglican Evangelicals: Protestant Secessions from the Via Media, c. 1800-1850* (Oxford: Oxford University Press, 2001), xvii

2 Patrick Collinson, *The Elizabethan Puritan Movement* (Oxford: Clarendon Press, 1967).

a congregational style outside the established system. As Michael Watts puts it in his history of dissenters, "The bishops, he came to believe, had so polluted the church that a new beginning had to be made."[3] So he tried to implement purer forms of church governance, at St Helen's, Bishopgate (in Norwich) and other places in East Anglia.

Browne's idea was that authority in the church should come from a mutual contract (or membership agreement) between members and elders. He was, however, arrested and twice imprisoned for preaching at illegal conventicles, and decided in the end that to pursue his goal of purity he would have to leave the country and go to the Netherlands. There was trouble within the congregation, however, and fights about whether the children of believers could be considered members of the church or not. Internal dissension broke up the new experimental church.

Things didn't go very well for Browne, so he left and went to Scotland, but found the Presbyterians there were worse than English bishops. So he returned to England, pretty disillusioned. He eventually came back into the Church of England. He taught in a school for a few years and was then instituted as Rector of a village church in Northamptonshire, and wrote against some of those "schismatical persons" who had carried through his earlier ideas more consistently. All was fine then for about a quarter of a century, until his nonconformity within the Church saw him suspended and eventually excommunicated. After he punched a policeman (!), he was imprisoned, and died in 1633.[4]

We might contrast Browne with Arthur Hildersham (1563-1632), who was also a Puritan around the same time, but not a separatist. He had some sympathy with Browne. The Brownists were right about "the general increase of all filthy and abominable sins in the land", he said, which made it right to fear that the candlestick (i.e. God's presence) was being taken away from England.[5] He thought a different system of government for the church might be

3 Michael Watts, *The Dissenters: From the Reformation to the French Revolution* (Oxford: Clarendon Press, 1978), 28.

4 See Watts, *Dissenters*, 28-34.

5 Arthur Hildersham, CVIII *Lectures upon the Fourth of John* (London, 1629), 165.

better, but he was prepared to live within what he saw as a flawed organisation so that he could continue to preach the gospel. In her excellent recent biography of Hildersham, Lesley Rowe puts it well:

> *Hildersham faced the difficult choice of whether to leave the Church of England or to remain within it. He recognized its flaws and corruptions but reckoned that as long as gospel preaching continued, this was a sign that God was still present in the church. His decision brought criticism from both sides: from the separatists, who argued that he lacked the courage to follow his convictions to their logical conclusion and leave an unbiblical organization, and from conformists, who regarded him as a troublemaker refusing to submit to lawful authority. Deciding to stay within the Church of England was not an easy option for Hildersham, for it brought years of suspension from ministry and suffering. Although some of the issues may be different now, evangelicals within the Church of England face a similar dilemma today.* [6]

Puritans continued to have a rocky time in the Church of England at some points, and they had to work hard to maintain their position. Elsewhere, I have looked in some detail at how St Antholin's church in London, and others like it, promoted the cause of gospel preaching which Hildersham had espoused in his day.[7] The real crunch point came, however, after the Puritan successes of the civil war and Commonwealth period evaporated with the Restoration of the monarchy in 1660. So we come, now to the tragedy of 1662.

The Tragedy of 1662

Actually, the so-called "Great Ejection" of ministers, many of them puritans,

6 Lesley A. Rowe, *The Life and Times of Arthur Hildersham: Prince Among Puritans* (Grand Rapids: Reformation Heritage Books, 2013), 177.

7 Lee Gatiss, "To Satisfy the People's Hunger for the Word: St. Antholin's as the Prototype Puritan Lectureship" in Gatiss (ed.), *Pilgrims, Warriors, and Servants: Puritan Wisdom for Today's Church. St. Antholin's Lectures, Volume 1: 1991-2000* (London: Latimer Trust, 2010), 3-22; and Lee Gatiss, "The Grand Nursery of Puritanism: St. Antholin's as a Strategic Centre for Gospel Ministry" in *Preachers, Pastors, and Ambassadors: St Antholin's Lectures, Volume 2: 2001-2010* (London: Latimer Trust, 2011), 3-45.

began in 1660. The 1660 Act for Confirming and Restoring of Ministers saw the ejection of 695 clergy from their posts, which were restored to their previous incumbents, if they were still alive. This undid some of the ejections that had taken place under Cromwell and earlier. It also ejected Baptists. Many of those ejected in 1660, however, managed to find other livings fairly quickly, and it was not intended to permanently remove most of them, just to restore and rearrange a few things.

However, in 1662, the Act of Uniformity led to the more substantial removal of 936 ministers.[8] The Act of Uniformity laid down that to be a minister, one must:

1. Be episcopally ordained, or re-ordained. This was unacceptable to many ordained during the previous two decades when there had not been any bishops legally operating in the country.

2. Give "unfeigned assent and consent to all and everything contained and prescribed" in the Book of Common Prayer. This was a much more egregious form of subscription than had previously been demanded, giving the BCP an aura of infallibility. And some of the changes in the new book seemed like a slap in the face to the Puritans. What's more, many of them could not have even seen the newly revised BCP before the date when their subscription was required.

3. They must renounce oaths taken during the Civil War and Commonwealth period, and promise never to try and change anything in the government of church or state. This, obviously, was unacceptable to many who had taken those oaths, such as the Solemn League and Covenant, and to those who might not feel the new settlement was unerringly perfect.

4. Declare that it was never lawful to *take up arms against the king, and that anyone who did so in the past was wrong.*

So it was not simply a matter of "Do you believe the gospel, or not?"—those

8 See the careful calculations in A. G. Matthews, *Calamy Revised: Being a Revision of Edmund Calamy's Account of the Ministers and Others Ejected and Silenced*, 1660-2 (Oxford: Clarendon Press, 1934), xii-xiii.

who did, left, and those who rejected it stayed in a compromised church. It was much more complex and contextual than that, though of course there were gospel issues bound up in some of these things.[9]

1662 was widely seen as a defeat for Puritanism, which was seriously persecuted in various ways for the next 25 years. However, the Reformed faith itself, in the sense of the church's underlying doctrine, was not defeated; the *Thirty-nine Articles* were not tampered with, and there were many solidly Reformed men serving the church and the academy under Charles II, as Stephen Hampton has shown in his book *Anti-Arminians*.[10]

About 10% of those ejected by the Acts of 1660 and 1662 did in fact later conform and find a way back into the Church of England. One of those was Dr. Thomas Horton, a notable Puritan theologian who had been Vice Chancellor of Cambridge when John Owen was Vice Chancellor of Oxford. He was removed as President of Queens' College, Cambridge in 1660, when his predecessor returned to the country, and silenced in 1662. Yet in 1666 he returned to the Church of England to fill a three-year interregnum at a place called St Helen's, Bishopsgate in the City of London. A contemporary account describes this as a large and wealthy congregation of half-conformists.[11]

Horton served St Helen's from that summer where almost all the other churches in the City burned down, until his death in 1673. Many of his sermons were published, and in them we can clearly see that Dr. Horton was a theologian of impeccable Reformed credentials who clearly preached predestination, penal substitution, particular atonement, promiscuous gospel preaching to all, and the necessity of the new birth.[12] And yet, he happily served in the Church of England.

The point is, many left in 1662 because they could not sign up for the new

9 For more on all this, see Lee Gatiss, *The Tragedy of 1662: The Ejection and Persecution of the Puritans* (London: Latimer Trust, 2007).

10 Stephen Hampton, *Anti-Arminians: The Reformed Tradition from Charles II to George I* (Oxford: Oxford University Press, 2008).

11 See Gatiss, *The Tragedy of 1662*, 46.

12 See Thomas Horton, *Forty-six Sermons upon the Whole Eighth Chapter of the Epistle of the Apostle Paul to the Romans* (London, 1674), e.g. pages 7, 9, 13, 14, 50, 501-503.

terms and conditions required for ministers in the Church of England. But not everyone did—William Gurnall, author of *The Christian in Complete Armour* was another who did not leave.[13] And some who were forced out, managed to come back in various ways later. Most of those ejected in 1662 did not leave the country. Only about 30 or 40 did so. Nonconformity from this point on means "not in the Church of England", whereas before it was possible to not conform on some things and still be within the Church.

Ten years after the ejection, there was a chance to see how the dissenters were doing. In 1672, there was a royal Indulgence which allowed nonconformists to meet openly if they registered their ministers and places of worship. About 850 were licensed as Presbyterians, 375 as Congregationalists, and 200 as Baptists. Now, there had been other ejections in the reigns of Mary, Elizabeth, James I, and during the Commonwealth. But none bore such permanent fruit as this one in 1660-1662, which as A. G. Matthew's puts it, "resulted in the rise of organised Dissent, which has been and still is a notable actor in English religious life."[14]

The ejection was not in some ways a secession, a voluntary leaving of the established church on a point of principle or theology. Technically, it was a legally enforced removal by way of a change of subscription standards. The impetus to divide did not come from the leavers, but from the remainers, so to speak. Yet its effect was more structurally disruptive and permanent than any voluntary secession.

Everything changed with the Toleration Act of 1689, which permitted legal toleration of non-Anglican churches on the basis that their ministers subscribe to most of the Thirty-nine Articles.[15] This is essentially what the Puritans had tried to achieve in Parliament in 1571 with An Act to Reform Certain Disorders touching Ministers of the Church, which prescribed assent

---

13 See the biography of Gurnall in J.C. Ryle, *Christian Leaders of the Seventeenth Century* (edited by Lee Gatiss; London: Lost Coin, 2015), 111–164.

14 See Matthews, *Calamy Revised*, xv-xvi.

15 With the exception of Article 34 ("On the Traditions of the Church"), Article 35 ("Of Homilies"), Article 36 ("Of Consecration of Bishops and Ministers"), and the first sentence of Article 20 ("The Church hath power to decree Rites and Ceremonies, and authority in Controversies of Faith.").

"to all the articles of religion, which only concern the confession of the true Christian faith and the doctrine of the sacraments."

Where you draw the boundaries and how you set subscription can have a huge impact. If the Puritans had been successful in 1571, the civil war may never have happened.

The Non-Jurors

A significant group of Anglicans left the established church because of the accession of William and Mary in 1688, which they thought was illegal. They were known as the Non-Jurors, because they could not swear an oath to the new monarchs. This was a serious institutional split. The non-jurors counted among their number the Archbishop of Canterbury himself, and 8 other diocesan bishops, several of whom had also stood up to James II when he had declared toleration for Roman Catholics.[16] There were also about 400 clergy. In 1690 they were deprived and deposed. The Episcopal Church of Scotland was almost entirely nonjuring as well, since it sided with the Jacobite cause politically.

It didn't take long before there was a split in 1717 over the proposed introduction of the mixed chalice, prayers of epiclesis and eucharistic oblation or "offering to God", prayers for the dead and so on, which some wanted to include in the Non-Jurors' new Book of Common Prayer. Nonjuring clergy and congregations declined throughout the eighteenth century, especially as the cause of the Stuart dynasty to which it had become attached also declined. It practically died out when Cardinal Henry Benedict Stuart became the Stuart heir in 1788—though not before the non-juring Scottish Episcopal Church had consecrated the first American bishop, Samuel Seabury in 1784. The story of how the Protestant Episcopal Church in the United States of America became TEC, is for another day. But note the connection.[17]

Around 1720, some Non-Jurors were seeking to affiliate with the Ortho-

16 See the laudatory chapter on them in J.C. Ryle, *Christian Leaders of the Seventeenth Century*, 165-202.

17 See, however, A. Guelzo, "The Reformed Episcopalians: Restoring Some Old Paths" in *Churchman* 104 (1990), on the disputed origins of American episcopalianism.

dox churches of the East, in an interesting attempt to provide international back-up to what you could say was their principled movement against pragmatic politics in the church. Some Non-Jurors such as Thomas Ken and William Law were quite influential, through their writings.[18] William Law's *A Serious Call to a Devout and Holy Life* (1728) was extremely influential among early Methodists and evangelicals, as well as Cardinal Newman.

Methodists and Evangelicals

There isn't space to consider the Methodist schism in any great detail. Needless to say that the vast majority of English evangelicals in the 18th century were firmly and decidedly Church of England. As I have shown elsewhere, George Whitefield was keen to demonstrate how Anglican his doctrine was,[19] and others such as Augustus Toplady, William Romaine, and James Hervey were also solidly Reformed and positively Anglican.[20]

John Wesley was not Reformed in his theological convictions at all, as I have recently demonstrated.[21] But he rejected the idea and tactic of secession because, he said, "the experiment has been so frequently tried already, and the success has never lived up to the expectation."[22] In this he was no doubt correct. Nevertheless, he decided to break from the Church of England by ordaining ministers himself, for America in 1784. This irregular act eventually led to an entirely separate denomination of Methodists. At the time of Wesley's death there were over 500 Methodist preachers in the British colonies and the United States.[23] Total membership of the Methodist societies

---

18 See Hugh A. L. Rice, *Thomas Ken: Bishop and Non-Juror* (London: SPCK, 1958).

19 See Lee Gatiss, "The Anglican Evangelist: George Whitefield" in Gatiss (ed.), *Positively Anglican: Building on the Foundations and Transforming the Church* (London: Lost Coin, 2016), 27-41.

20 See Lee Gatiss, *The True Profession of the Gospel: Augustus Toplady and Reclaiming our Reformed Foundations* (London: Latimer Trust, 2009).

21 Lee Gatiss, "Strangely Warmed: John Wesley's Arminian Campaigns" in my *Cornerstones of Salvation: Foundations and Debates in the Reformed Tradition* (Welwyn: Evangelical Press, 2017), 202-229.

22 John Wesley, *Reasons Against a Separation from the Church of England* (London, 1758).

23 See Kenneth Hylson-Smith, *Evangelicals in the Church of England 1734-1984* (Edinburgh: T&T Clark, 1988), 17-21.

in Britain was recorded as 56,000 in 1791, rising to 360,000 in 1836 and 1,463,000 by the national census of 1851. Today it is a worldwide denomination, although declining in the UK and USA.

Secession doesn't always grow that way. In the 17th century many who left the Church of England ended up as Unitarians, especially those who were decidedly against systematic theology, creeds, and confessions and wanted to only talk about and study the Bible. They soon dwindled in number. In the 18th century, the Countess of Huntingdon's Connexion was also detached, along with some Methodists.[24]

In the 19th century, various individuals left the Church of England because they didn't like infant baptism. The Free Church of England people began to leave, to try and secure a purified and free "true Anglicanism", in the middle of the nineteenth century.[25] In the 20th century, with the influence of Martyn Lloyd-Jones and others, some left the Church of England for Congregationalism and other nonconformist groups in the 1960s and 1970s.[26] When John Stott addressed the Church Society conference in 1965 he said,

> *Some evangelicals of the Free Churches are talking of seceding from their different Churches in order to form a United Evangelical Church. I, for one, ardently hope they will not do so. I believe that history as well as Scripture is against them, and I am quite sure that they would not carry more than a small handful of Anglican Evangelicals with them.*[27]

Part of Stott's biblical argument was that "the remnant was within the Church not outside it."[28]

---

24 See Richard Turnbull, *Transformed Heart, Transforming Church: the Countess of Huntingdon's Connexion* (London: Latimer Trust, 2015).

25 See John Fenwick, *The Free Church of England: Introduction to an Anglican Tradition* (London: T&T Clark Continuum, 2004).

26 See Andrew Atherstone, "Lloyd-Jones and the Anglican Secession Crisis" in Andrew Atherstone and David Ceri Jones (eds.), *Engaging with Martyn Lloyd-Jones: The Life and Legacy of 'the Doctor* (Nottingham: Apollos, 2011), 261-292.

27 Quoted in Alister Chapman, "John R. W. Stott and English Evangelicalism, 1938-84" (PhD Thesis, University of Cambridge, 2004), 141.

28 See Timothy Dudley-Smith, *John Stott: A Global Ministry* (Leicester: IVP, 2001), 67-68. The fact that "remnant" theology was such an important component of the argument on both sides at this point, is one of the reasons we have included a chapter on it in this

His prediction was right: there was never more than a gentle drip of evangelicals leaving the Church of England for nonconformity (about 20 between 1964-1974),[29] though some of them were influential.[30] Some years later, after the ordination of women was passed in 1992, the Church of England (Continuing) was formed. This attempted a structural solution to secession, though again, it did not attract many to leave.

Where are they now? Thinking of those who left in the 18th century, about 1000 people meet each week still in the Countess of Huntingdon's churches. From the 19th century secessions, the Free Church of England is still around, though it is still small, and generally much more high church than many evangelicals would be comfortable with; indeed, two bishops and ten evangelical congregations within it formed an internally dissenting Evangelical Connexion in 2003. Of those who left the established church in the 20th century, the Church of England (Continuing) may not continue for very much longer. It has less than a handful of congregations faithfully soldiering on with the King James Version and the 1662 Prayer Book. There are also a few ministers still going of the 20 or so who left the Church of England after Martyn Lloyd-Jones called for more evangelical unity in the 1960s. I met one recently who had once been a curate at our church in Cambridge, and he was still pleased that he had made that move. God seemed to have blessed his later ministry.

Much good gospel work was done by seceders, and some felt liberated by their uncoupling from the established church. They took a stand as their consciences dictated, and because of how they saw things going in the national church. It is neither right nor safe to act against conscience, as Martin Luther once famously said! God alone is Lord of the conscience, as the Westminster Confession declares (chapter 20). The fact that not many joined the later

---

present book.

29 According to Atherstone, "Lloyd-Jones and the Anglican Secession Crisis", 262. Whether this number is indicative of a "crisis" or not, it was certainly a live issue in evangelical discussions.

30 See e.g. Herbert Carson, *Farewell to Anglicanism* (Worthing: Henry E. Walter, 1969). When Carson left the Church of England he became an assistant minister at Lloyd-Jones's Westminster Chapel.

secessionists, in comparison to Methodism or the Non-Juror group for example, does not mean their work was a "failure" or insignificant in the eyes of God, whose "power is made perfect in weakness" (2 Corinthians 12:9).[31] Yet it does indicate that for something to last beyond the lifetime of charismatic and energetic leaders, an institutional structure and a critical mass of individuals (including bishops) seems to be necessary. I say this as a historical observation, and a recommendation for those who would secede well, not as a command against it or any kind of value judgment. Whether it is a wise course of action or not in any particular circumstance, lasting secession seems to require planned institutional succession.

I'm not sure anyone can blame those wanting to start out from scratch away from the Church of England, when we can all see a lamentable credibility gap between the rhetoric of careful synodical statements and the incessant official frowns (and worse) which many of us have had to endure. Sensitive and insecure critics within the establishment may like to keep that in mind when they struggle to tolerate these enterprising souls, some of whom are labouring in places where less than 1% of people currently go to church. The most important thing is that Christ is proclaimed, and in that we rejoice!

However, the "Chexit dividend" may not be as great as some imagine. I still think there is wisdom in what J. C. Ryle said, after a spate of secessions in his day:

> *It is not so sure as it seems that we mend matters by leaving the Church of England. Every man knows the faults of his own house, but he never knows the faults of another till he moves into it, and then perhaps he finds he is worse off than he was before his move. There are often smoky chimneys, and bad drains, and draughts, and doors that will not shut, and windows that will not open, in No. 2 as well as in No. 1. All is not perfect among Dissenters and Plymouth Brethren. We may find to our cost, if*

31 Cf. the reflection of Darryl Hart that "Reformed communions that put a premium on theological consistency may have to accept that they will always be numerically small" (and the surrounding context) in my *Christianity and the Tolerance of Liberalism: J. Gresham Machen and the Presbyterian Controversy of 1922-1937* (London: Latimer Trust, 2008), 70-71

> *we join them in disgust with the Church of England, that we have only changed one sort of evil for another, and that the chimney smokes in chapel as well as in church… So long as we have truth, liberty, and an unaltered Confession of faith in the Church of England, so long I am convinced that the way of patience is much better than the way of secession."*[32]

The case for remaining is still strong.[33]

Conclusions

Briefly, then, as I close, here are 12 conclusions we may draw from the history of Anglican secessions:

1. There have always been some who leave, for reasons of conscience, theology, or strategy.
2. There have always been good people who stayed.
3. Infant baptism was often an issue, or other issues such as Arminianism.
4. So were alternative ecclesiologies (Presbyterian, Congregationalist) which suggested secession.
5. Leavers can accuse remainers of a lack of courage.
6. Remaining is not an easy life, and remainers often agree with leavers about the parlous state of the C of E.
7. Leaving is not easy, especially in terms of succession, unity, and long-term institution building.
8. The cause of leaving will not always be straightforward, but may separate friends and allies.
9. Conscience and strategic judgment may lead people with similar theology to do different things.

---

32 J. C. Ryle, *Knots Untied: Being plain statements on disputed points in Religion from the standpoint of an Evangelical Churchman* (London: James Clarke, 1964), 148-149.

33 See the excellent case put by James Taylor, "Sticking With It: Believing in the Church of England" in Gatiss (ed.), *Positively Anglican*, 11-25.

10. We must be wary of any changes to de facto or de jure standards of subscription.

11. There's a cost to secession.

12. Secession can undermine the stand of those who stay.

Should we stay or should we go? Well, this chapter is only about the history. The future is something else and, unlike some, I claim no prophetic gift or special spiritual insight about that!

Lee Gatiss *is the Director of Church Society and Lecturer in Church History at Union School of Theology.*

Chapter 6

Flourishing in a Hostile World

How the Early Church did it

Lee Gatiss

In this final chapter, we will look at how the early church flourished and grew in the midst of persecution and heresy. The church grew from the tiny seed of a handful of believers in the upper room in Jerusalem, to conquer the Roman Empire in two and a half centuries, and many other parts of the world too. And this despite it having no armies at its command, in a context where Christians were a despised and marginalised minority who appeared extreme to those around them—and where the mainstream church of Jesus Christ was assailed by satanic attempts to subvert the truth of its gospel with various seemingly attractive false teachings.

The resonance is obvious: we too live in a time where the majority culture around us is hostile to the gospel in so many ways. We may not face the prospect of going to a literal stake or to the lions for what we believe, but there is ignorance and incomprehension, scorn and derision—and there are often difficult choices to be made between the dictates of Christian conscience and the demands of a modern career or profession. Not only that, but within the church itself there is outright hostility to the truth of the Bible in some places, and open opposition to historic orthodoxy, both doctrinal and moral.

Those were all things faced by the early church in the first 300 years of our era, until the days of Emperor Constantine the Great. And yet, the church at the beginning of the 4th century was on the cusp of its most spectacular success. By the end of that century it was the official religion of the Roman Empire.

I am not claiming that this is what we have to look forward to in the century before us. I have no prophetic insight into that. I do not claim to have any extraordinary spiritual perception that enables me to predict the future with great confidence or give infallible advice on how we should act today. But what I do have is the Bible, and some lessons that we might draw from the history of those early days, which might help us as we come to grips with a situation very different from that facing the church of our grandfathers.

Let's begin by looking at the Bible, and an account of gospel growth in Acts 11:19-30:

> *Now those who were scattered because of the persecution that arose over Stephen traveled as far as Phoenicia and Cyprus and Antioch, speaking the word to no one except Jews. But there were some of them, men of Cyprus and Cyrene, who on coming to Antioch spoke to the Hellenists also, preaching the Lord Jesus. And the hand of the Lord was with them, and a great number who believed turned to the Lord. The report of this came to the ears of the church in Jerusalem, and they sent Barnabas to Antioch. When he came and saw the grace of God, he was glad, and he exhorted them all to remain faithful to the Lord with steadfast purpose, for he was a good man, full of the Holy Spirit and of faith. And a great many people were added to the Lord. So Barnabas went to Tarsus to look for Saul, and when he had found him, he brought him to Antioch. For a whole year they met with the church and taught a great many people. And in Antioch the disciples were first called Christians.*
>
> *Now in these days prophets came down from Jerusalem to Antioch. And one of them named Agabus stood up and foretold by the Spirit that there would be a great famine over all the world (this took place in the days of Claudius). So the disciples determined, every one according to his ability, to send relief to the brothers living in Judea. And they did so, sending it to*

the elders by the hand of Barnabas and Saul.

We can quickly draw out six key points from Luke's account of the growth of the early church here. First, it appears that persecution helps the church to grow. We do not have to like it. It is never pleasant. But it can still achieve the purposes of God. The persecutions in Acts, for example, always seem to result in Christians being scattered further and further away from ground zero, and Jesus's words are fulfilled: "you will be my witnesses in Jerusalem, and in all Judea and Samaria, and to the ends of the earth" (Acts 1:8). It may have been in chains, but Paul reached Rome. It may have been in a position of great weakness, but he preached the gospel before Caesar, the most powerful man in the world.

Second, as it goes, the gospel breaks boundaries. It went first to the Jews and then to the gentiles, as we see in this passage. Not only that, but it also unites Jews and Gentiles along the way, overriding every other marker of human identity and commanding the loyalty of all it converts.

Third, the gospel triumphed because "the hand of the Lord was with them." The flourishing of the good news does not depend merely on our hard work, our political acumen, or the grace and favour of the world, the press, or the establishment. Barnabas saw what "the grace of God" had done.

Fourth, the word does the work. The people involved are said to spread the word, tell the good news, and to teach the people. That is how the church grows: as the word of God is preached and taught. The Bible is sufficient. No extra, special techniques are required to encourage people in the face of heresy and persecution, "to remain faithful to the Lord with steadfast purpose."

Fifth, key individuals can be useful and play a part: Barnabas and Saul were mighty instruments in God's hands to bring many to faith and strengthen them in it during those very early days. But so were the unnamed "men of Cyprus and Cyrene" who saw a great number of people turn to the Lord. In either case, the glory and the credit were Christ's alone.

Finally, we can see in this passage that the early Christians applied their faith and helped each other out. When famine came, the predominantly Gentile church in Antioch sent vital relief to the Jewish church in Jerusalem. They loved one another, and showed their unity in Christ through acts of love and deeds of faith.

This is how the church grew and multiplied in the first few decades. And indeed, that is how it continued to multiply and spread for the next couple of centuries. In their monographs on the growth of the early church, the secular methodology of Rodney Stark and Bart Ehrman, for some reason, discounts the possibility that Acts is telling the truth. They think it impossible that 3000 people were converted at Pentecost, and that Acts 4:4 must be wrong to say there were 5000 believers. So they start out by saying there were only 20 Christians when Jesus died and about 8000 by the end of the first century. A tiny number.

But projecting the statistics forward as best they can on the available data, they say that by the time of Constantine, the church had reached about 10% of the population. And there were about 30 million Christians in the Roman Empire by the middle of the 4th century. That's over 50% of the population—a staggering number, which is within the range of many other historians too.[1]

How has this amazing growth—from nothing to official majority religion of the empire—been explained? Obviously we can say that Christianity spread because it was the true faith. We can say that the triumph of the gospel was prophesied and commanded by Jesus, and so it was bound to come to pass. God did it. Jesus is King and he subdues the earth.

These are all good and right and true things to say. But it didn't have to happen this way. The triumph of the church in only three centuries was not inevitable. Apart from the obvious theological reasons we might adduce for the success of the true gospel, how else have people explained the remarkable success of the church up to Constantine? Sociologists such as Rodney Stark, and historians such as, most recently, Bart Ehrman have written on this. I think we can boil down what they have said about the rise of Christianity

---

1 See Rodney Stark, *The Rise of Christianity: How the Obscure, Marginal Jesus Movement Became the Dominant Religious Force in the Western World in a Few Centuries* (San Francisco: HarperOne, 1997), 3-27, and Bart D. Ehrman, *The Triumph of Christianity: How a Forbidden Religion Swept the World* (London: OneWorld, 2018), 160-177.

into seven points.

The church was evangelistic, exclusive, all-encompassing (that is, it made demands on your entire life), and eternity-focused. The endurance of the martyrs played a major role, as did the embrace of authentic community. Finally, the early church was an excluding church—it dealt effectively with major heretical threats to its integrity and cohesion, and did not practice what is nowadays called "good disagreement"—the relativising of truth and the exaltation of unity at any cost.

Let's look at that those seven points a little further.

1. The church was evangelistic.

One of the interesting things about Rodney Stark's calculations and Bart Ehrman's tweaking of those, is that we come out with a figure of around 40% growth in the church per decade on average, up to the end of the 4th century. Because the early church was an evangelistic church. Its doctrine of Christ's second coming to judge the living and the dead encouraged keen evangelism. The zeal of the early Christians was such that they were enthusiastic about sharing their faith. That's why they grew.

But those numbers are actually not ridiculous or even perhaps "miraculous" when we consider that they basically amount to this: every church of about 100 people making 3 or 4 converts per year. As Stark says, "the rise of Christianity required no miraculous rates of conversion."[2] The Mormons have achieved the same sort of growth curve without the need for miraculous mass conversions (or truth on their side!).

This evangelism was of course aided by the Pax Romana—the ability to travel along Roman roads guaranteed by Roman soldiers anywhere in the vast Roman Empire. It was also aided by the fact that there was a common language throughout much of the empire—the Greek spread by Alexander the Great's short-lived though vast empire which had preceded Rome. It was also aided by the fact that the Jews had spread all over the Empire, and provided a convenient first base for many evangelistic efforts: as Paul said, "first for the

2 Stark, *The Rise of Christianity*, 12.

Jews, then for the Gentiles"—and there were millions of Jews all over the place.

Yet this consistent evangelistic effort was not sustained by an army of wandering missionaries, though there were some itinerant preachers here and there. It wasn't all done by big celebrities holding open air rallies and appearing on TV. It mostly happened through ordinary means, gossiping the gospel to neighbours and bringing up children to know and love the Lord.

Kenneth Scott Latourette says, "the chief agent in the expansion of Christianity appears not to have been those who made it a profession or made it a major part of their occupation, but men and women who carried on their livelihood in some purely secular manner and spoke of their faith to those they met in this natural fashion."[3] Or as Michael Green puts it, "Communicating the faith was not regarded as the preserve of the very zealous or of the officially designated evangelist. Evangelism was the prerogative and the duty of every Church member... The ordinary people of the Church saw it as their job: Christianity was supremely a lay movement, spread by informal missionaries."[4]

So lesson number one from the early church is that we must retain this edge in our own day, if we are to flourish in the midst of a culture that knows nothing of our faith in Christ and him crucified. We have far better means of travel and communication these days, even than the Romans, and there are a million ways to get the message out. Christianity first spread through natural social networks and lines of communication, and so Christians today must use all the means of publishing, broadcasting, and social networking to engage the world around us with the good news of our Saviour Jesus Christ.[5] But above all, each of us has at our disposal what Stark calls "the best of all market-place techniques: person-to-person influence."[6] We must make the most of our natural relationships with those who don't know Jesus.

---

3 K. S. Latourette, *A History of the Expansion of Christianity. Volume 1: The First Five Centuries* (New York: Harper & Brothers, 1937), 116.

4 Michael Green, *Evangelism in the Early Church* (London: Hodder & Stoughton, 1984), 332.

5 See Stark, *The Rise of Christianity*, 18 and Ehrman, *The Triumph of Christianity*, 119 on social networks.

6 Stark, *The Rise of Christianity*, 208.

Here's a question to to chew on, however: Christianity is said to have "triumphed" in the Roman Empire when it reached about 10% around 312 AD or 56% of the population around 350 AD. The last UK census showed that of our population (around the same size as the Roman Empire in total), more than 59% ticked "Christian" as their religion. Why is that not considered "successful"? Discussing that would be a revealing exercise, and help us understand our own preconceptions and assumptions about "success."

2. The church was exclusive.

Second, the early church was not just evangelistic. It was also exclusive. Edward Gibbon says in *The Decline and Fall of the Roman Empire* that one of the prime reasons for the rapid growth of the church was "the inflexible, and, if we may use the expression, the intolerant zeal of the Christians."[7] They were convinced they were right, and other gods and religions were not. Unlike devotees of the pagan gods, Christians were expected to become devoted to one god alone and abstain from other cultic practices. This is one of the main reasons Christianity took over the empire. "One might think," says Ehrman, "this exclusionary insistence would be off-putting and offensive in a world filled with gods, dooming the Christian mission to failure. On the contrary, it had just the opposite effect. It was this claim that led to the triumph of Christianity."[8]

There was unparalleled novelty in this approach, which shocked the pagan world of ancient Greece and Rome. Every convert to Christianity was a loss to the pagan world. The old gods were destroyed as Christianity advanced, which was not true when people simply changed allegiance from one pagan god or goddess to another, in a pluralistic culture which was happy with huge diversity. If Christianity had been evangelistic but not exclusive, it may have made some converts, but it would have been subsumed along with other pluralistic practices, and paganism would not have been affected. Christ would just have been added to the pantheon of gods you could worship. The very exclusivity of salvation in Christ alone is what helped to preserve the Church.[9]

7 Edward Gibbon, *The History of the Decline and Fall of the Roman Empire: Volume 2* (Basil: Tourneisen, 1789), 221 (chapter 15).

8 Ehrman, *The Triumph of Christianity*, 115-116.

9 Cf. Ehrman, *The Triumph of Christianity*, 125.

So a pluralistic culture that disliked exclusive truth claims was not necessarily detrimental for the gospel. Neither is our pluralistic culture an excuse for us to keep quiet and not keep speaking the truth. Preaching "only one way to salvation", attracted followers, and depleted the ranks of paganism as it did so. That was the precise culture in which Christianity grew, and it grew not by radical inclusion and unconditional affirmation of everything and everyone, but by virtue of its unique and exclusive claims.

3. The church was all-encompassing

Related to this, a third reason for the success of Christianity, is that it is an all-encompassing religion, that made demands on one's entire life. It was not simply about adding a god to your personal pantheon, or changing which deity you burnt incense to. It was about changing your whole life. This was not how ancient religions worked usually.[10] Christianity was totalising, in a way that worshipping Artemis or Zeus was not. So, says Ehrman, "since Christians conceptualised their religion as a coherent system, they began thinking that everything outside their religion was a competing coherent system."[11] Paganism became an —ism, with thousands of varieties, all opposed to the one truth. This enabled the opposition to be more effectively attacked and portrayed as unethical.

This also meant that Christianity created a loyalty in its adherents, which extended over their whole lives. It created a new identity in believers. Followers of Apollo or Venus did not make their choice of deity into their most important characteristic. One did not "come out" as a Venusian or a worshipper of Mars. You just added that to your existing life, without importing much in the way of ethical or doctrinal demands. It did not create a common bond between Mars believers, so to speak. But believing in Christ did, and believing in Christ came with an ethical claim over every second of your day and night, and a set of orthodox doctrinal beliefs.

We see how attractive this sort of identity-making is in our own society.

---

10 See Augustine, *The City of God*, 2.6 on how pagan gods did not demand holiness of life in their followers.

11 Ehrman, *The Triumph of Christianity*, 127.

Once people define themselves by their sexuality or by some other marker of difference, it is very difficult to shake their loyalty to that thing, which becomes a "cause" and a basic marker of who they are in their own minds. Our modern societies have a number of competing, totalising narratives which people are asked to buy into. Many of them are aggressively evangelistic and jealously exclusive.

That may make our evangelism today much more of an existential challenge in some ways. But the lesson we learn from the early church is that we don't make progress by abandoning the exclusivity and all-encompassing nature of the gospel.

4. The church was eternity-focused

Next, the early church was focused on eternity. Edward Gibbon claimed that the doctrine of immortality was one of the main causes of the rapid growth of the Christian church. Pagans were desperate he said, to learn about the possibility of an afterlife. Bart Ehrman also makes the point in his book *The Triumph of Christianity* that Christian eschatology was one of the distinctive things about those who follow Jesus compared to the pagan environment of the first century. Christians had a clear view of a judgment day to come. They believed in the torments of hell for those who don't believe, and the joys of a heavenly utopia for those who remain steadfast in their faith in Jesus.

Not so with paganism. Bart Ehrman says, "most pagans appear not to have subscribed to the idea of any afterlife whatsoever."[12] So Christians put forward their novel theory, creating a problem for their hearers (you're going to hell) and then provided a satisfying solution: salvation in Christ. This was, says Ehrman "effective propaganda." So heaven is nice as a promise for downtrodden slaves and others who struggle in this world, while the terrors and horrors of hell can be used to put the literal fear of God into unbelievers, and frighten them into the arms of Jesus. Stark also says that the need for potent compensations for scarce rewards is a reason why more this-worldly faiths do not attract the less privileged.[13] I don't buy all the cynical rhetoric here. The

12 Ehrman, *The Triumph of Christianity*, 155.

13 Stark, *The Rise of Christianity*, 38.

Lord Jesus is the one who spoke most of eternal life and eternal punishment, in the Gospels, and I'm convinced he knew what he was talking about. But clearly, there is something in this observation that the eternal focus on the Christian message was extremely important for the early Christians and contributed to the success of their evangelism.

Surprisingly, this seemingly basic Christian doctrine is another thing which is under attack these days from the trendy liberal end of Protestantism. So Steve Chalke recently (April 2018) tweeted that, "Christianity is supposed to be not so much about life AFTER death as life BEFORE it, quality of life right here, right now, of which poverty and injustice rob so many." In January 2019, he also said, "I'm not as bothered about going to heaven when I die as I am about bringing a bit of heaven to earth right now". To which I reply (and did literally reply on Twitter): I hate poverty, war, and injustice. But the hope of a far better life beyond death, with the risen Lord Jesus, has always been absolutely central to the Christian message. The gospel is not mostly about improving "quality of life" in this fallen world, as important as that is.

That was something which was particularly important to those who suffered for their faith in the opening centuries of our era.

5. The church grew because of the endurance of the martyrs

The endurance of Christian martyrs was also something that attracted the attention and the admiration of many pagans. After all, Bart Ehrman asks, "how many martyrs for Zeus do we hear about?"[14] Nowadays we find it difficult to endure negative comments on Twitter. But they endured far worse, and it inspired and attracted people to our crucified God. Justin Martyr, an early Christian apologist, was a martyr himself; but he actually became a Christian in the first place because he, said, Christians' martyrdom showed him that they deserved to be believed.[15]

---

14 Ehrman, *The Triumph of Christianity*, 156.

15 See chapter 12 of his Second Apology, in Cleveland Coxe (ed.), *The Apostolic Fathers with Justin Martyr and Irenæus* (ANF1; Peabody, Massachusetts: Hendrickson, 1999), 192.

Does our behaviour in the midst of suffering and persecution do that, or does it put people off? As one second century Christian (Tertullian) put it, the blood of the martyrs is seed. But today, the way Christians often react under pressure from the world contains nothing of that vital sap which can turn hardened opponents into diehard believers. Somehow, however, the way Christians endured under such ultimate persecution persuaded some people to give their gospel a hearing. Some thought it was foolish, sheer stubbornness for Christians not to recant and live.[16] But others had their heads turned.

Now, that was the case even though the absolute number of people who died for their faith was actually very small. The vast majority of pagans never saw an actual Christian martyrdom. The stories were often enough. Rodney Stark says, "even the most brutal persecutions of Christians were haphazard and limited, and the state ignored thousands of persons who openly professed the new religion."[17] We were pretty free to get on with things despite official disrepute, for most of the time. Yet the fact that, when it came to it, Christians endured under torture or were willing to die for their faith in Christ, made Christianity a credible religion and placed a high potential value on it in other people's eyes.[18]

6. The church was an embracing community

One thing that many others would have experienced, however, is the embracing community of the Christian church. Authentic community is vital for local churches, even more than big celebrity Christian speakers and mass rallies and media appearances. That wasn't how they grew back then in the early days of the church. Rodney Stark however goes even further. He claims that the superior care experienced by Christians in the community of the church was one of the most significant factors in the church's growth. So much so that the major epidemics which killed off thousands of people in the ancient world helped the church become dominant, because Christians offered each other superior nursing care. Paganism, he says, had a "relative inability to confront

16 E.g. Marcus Aurelius, *Meditations* (trans. R. B. Rutherford; Oxford: Oxford University Press, 1989), 102.

17 Stark, *The Rise of Christianity*, 46.

18 Cf. Stark, *The Rise of Christianity*, 174.

these crises socially or spiritually."[19]

Stark (who is a sociologist) also sees superior fertility, because of Christian treatment of women and children, as statistically significant for church growth over time. And he says the new culture created by church communities were "capable of making life in Greco-Roman cities more tolerable" and therefore enabled growth in such environments. He concludes that "Paganism failed to develop the kind of voluntary system of good works that Christians had been constructing for more than three centuries; moreover, paganism lacked the religious ideas that would have made such organised efforts plausible."[20]

At the same time, "Pagan cults were not able to get people to do much of anything," says Stark, while commenting on "the inability of nonexclusive faiths to generate belonging."[21] Indeed, it is Christian doctrine which created Christian community, which was so powerful a factor in our early success: "Central doctrines of Christianity prompted and sustained attractive, liberating, and effective social relations and organisations." This was "the ultimate factor in the rise of Christianity."[22] The gospel brought "a new conception of humanity to a world saturated with capricious cruelty and the vicarious love of death."[23] It is still capable of doing so today, in our world—which is increasingly the same in its brutality, its worship of sex, and its casual use of violence as entertainment (in TV, films, and video games).

Notice what wasn't responsible for the rise of Christianity. The conversion of the emperor Constantine was not the cause of the growth of the church. It was, if anything, a response to it. After a while, the rate of growth slowed, once Christianity became the official religion of the empire. So the triumph of the faith wasn't achieved through political means, by securing the reins of power and the support of the state. Far from it. The church thrived without that. As we have also seen it do in China over the last century, of course. State support, freedom of speech, and freedom of religion may be great gifts

19 Stark, *The Rise of Christianity*, 74ff, 94. Ehrman, *The Triumph of Christianity*, 138ff is not so convinced.

20 Stark, *The Rise of Christianity*, 128, 162, 189.

21 Stark, *The Rise of Christianity*, 206.

22 Stark, *The Rise of Christianity*, 211.

23 Stark, *The Rise of Christianity*, 214.

and privileges. But they are by no means prerequisites for the growth of the church.

7. The church excluded some

One other aspect of early Christianity ought to be mentioned. It was an excluding faith. That is, it had to handle heresy and false teaching and work out how to draw a line around it. These things are inevitable, because counterfeits always spring up where there is something of real value. How did the early church handle heresy? By excluding it. They were keen to create clear boundaries between truth and error. Even in the face of hostility from the world and the surrounding culture, they did not relativise truth for the sake of some kind of unity.

We see this in the Bible itself. The apostle Paul, for example, exhorts the church to drive out the recalcitrantly immoral and avoid charlatans in the church (1 Corinthians 5; 2 Timothy 3).

The apostle John's letters urge congregations to discern between the Spirit of God and the spirit of Antichrist, and not to welcome those who bring false teaching (1 John 4:1-3; 2 John 9-10). The risen Lord Jesus himself commends churches for not tolerating wicked people who claim to be apostles but are not (Revelation 2:2), and commands them to repent quickly if they harbour those who teach false doctrine or immoral lifestyles (Revelation 2:14-16, 20).

Various heresies grew up to afflict the church. Gnosticism, Doceticism, Marcionism, Pelagianism, and Arianism for example. And the church had to decide whether these were issues on which they had to divide, or which they could decide to agree to disagree about.

I read recently of a bishop who said that, "If you must make a choice between heresy and schism, always choose heresy."[24] But institutional unity was not so highly valued above gospel truth in the early church. In the third century, Cyprian of Carthage advised that once a bishop joins a dodgy sect and preaches heresy, he should be excommunicated, and another elected to fill his

---

24 See J. B. Simmons, *The Awakening of Washington's Church: How a Church Lost Everything and Gained What Matters Most* (CreateSpace, 2016), 123.

place, because he has departed from the faith and unity of the church:

> *For what if any harbour in the sea shall begin to be mischievous and dangerous to ships, by the breach of its defences; do not the navigators direct their ships to other neighbouring ports where there is a safe and practicable entrance, and a secure station? Or if, on the road, any inn should begin to be beset and occupied by robbers, so that whoever should enter would be caught by the attack of those who lie in wait there; do not the travellers, as soon as this its character is discovered, seek other houses of entertainment on the road, which shall be safer, where the lodging is trustworthy, and the inns safe for the travellers? And this ought now to be the case with us, dearest brother, that we should receive to us with ready and kindly humanity our brethren, who, tossed on the rocks of Marcian [Marcianus of Arles, a Novatian heretic], are seeking the secure harbours of the Church."*[25]

Furthermore, says Cyprian: "people obedient to the Lord's precepts, and fearing God, ought to separate themselves from a sinful prelate, and not to associate themselves with the sacrifices of a sacrilegious priest, especially since they themselves have the power either of choosing worthy priests, or of rejecting unworthy ones."[26]

There are even more clear examples in the life of the great Athanasius. He was clear in opposing the heresy of Arianism and establishing orthodox Christology. He taught clearly that Christ is of one being or substance with the Father, and not of similar substance as the Arians said. Although the Arians said there was a time when Christ was not, Athanasius and others said Christ was the eternal God.

When the Emperor Constantine heard of this debate and that it was threatening the unity of the church of which he was now a member, he wrote the two sides a letter. He said, that they were "pertinaciously contend[ing] with one another about matters of small or scarcely the least importance." He asked them, "Is it right on account of insignificant and vain contentions between you about words, that brethren should be set in opposition against

---

25 Epistle 66.3 in Cleveland Coxe (ed.), *Fathers of the Third Century: Hippolytus, Cyprian, Caius, Novatian* (ANF5: Peabody, Massachusetts: Hendrickson, 1999), 368.

26 Epistle 67.3 in Coxe (ed.), *Fathers of the Third Century*, 370.

brethren; and that the honourable communion should be distracted by unhallowed dissension, through our striving with one another respecting things so unimportant, and by no means essential?" It was an "insignificant subject of controversy" he stated.[27]

Constantine wanted to unite the empire through his support for the church. But now the church was divided and threatened that very unity. As is often the case with new Christians, perhaps, he couldn't understand why it was so important to be precise about doctrine. He preferred some kind of "good disagreement" on this trivial and secondary matter (Christ's divinity!).

There were some who agreed, that the church should not engage in such subtle systematic theology, but just get on with straightforward faith and good works.[28] But as you probably know, the Council of 300 bishops which met at Nicaea was absolutely clear about the Arian heresy, and had no qualms about anathematising those who held to it. They did not think the basic Apostles' Creed was sufficient for the heresies of a later day. So they composed their own expanded version, to directly address the new problems. This eventually developed into the so-called Nicene Creed, which remains Anglican doctrine to this day.[29]

A compromise peace for the sake of unity and mission was never going to cut it. Athanasius's approach won the day—we must be clear on truth even if it excludes. Yet that did not happen easily. He was exiled a number of times and did not always appear to be on the winning side. When things were going badly, as Patriarch of Alexandria he even ordained orthodox people irregularly in places where Arianism had the upper hand. For example, we read that:

> *Immediately on his arrival in Egypt, Athanasius displaced those whom he knew to be attached to Arianism, and placed the government of the*

27 See Philip Schaff and Henry Wace (eds.), *Nicene and Post-Nicene Fathers: Volume 2. Socrates, Sozomenus: Church Histories* (NPNF2; Peabody, Massachusetts: Hendrickson, 1999), 6-7 (Socrates 1.7).

28 Socrates 1.8 (page 9): "a man of unsophisticated understanding reproved these reasoners, telling them that Christ and his apostles did not teach us dialectics, art, nor vain subtleties, but simple-mindedness, which is preserved by faith and good works."

29 See Canons A2 and A5, Article 8, and the *Book of Common Prayer.*

Church and the confession of the Nicaean council in the hands of those whom he approved, and he exhorted them to hold to this with earnestness. It was said at that time, that, when he was travelling through other countries, he effected the same change, if he happened to visit churches which were under the Arians. He was certainly accused of having dared to perform the ceremony of ordination in cities where he had no right to do so."[30]

Athanasius was not alone in this policy of irregular ordinations and working against the Arians.[31] Others did the same, appointing people to churches so that they might oppose the "official" bishops if they were Arian or otherwise unorthodox.

So we see that the early church flourished by keeping its doctrine as pure as possible on primary issues, despite official pressure from on high to compromise and get along for the sake of unity.

They were willing to risk personal discomfort and exile, and a messy ecclesiastical situation, for the sake of the truth about Jesus Christ which was enshrined and passed on for the spiritual health of future generations in the Nicene Creed.

Conclusion

In some ways, we could have simply looked at Acts 11, the passage with which I began, and drawn out lessons from there. But what I have tried to do, is not only see how the New Testament itself describes Christian growth in the middle of the first century, but continue the story into the next few generations as well.

Carried along by the Holy Spirit, Luke gives us a prophetic insight into the causes and progress of Christianity. Church historians and sociologists

30 P. Schaff and H. Wace (eds.), *Nicene and Post-Nicene Fathers: Second Series* (Peabody, Massachusetts: Hendrickson, 1999 [1899]), 2:299 in *The Ecclesiastical History of Sozomen*, 3:21. See also 2:53 (*The Ecclesiastical History of Socrates*, 2:24).

31 See similar actions and irregular ordinations in Theodoret's history of the church too, in *Nicene and Post-Nicene Fathers: Second Series*, 3:116, 133-134 (Theodoret, 4:12, 5:4). I am extremely grateful to Dr Mark S. Smith of Clare College, Cambridge for help with these patristic references.

cannot do that. But what they can do is reflect on the evidence that is left behind and humbly come to some tentative conclusions. My conclusion is that the church triumphed in the Roman Empire and became "the destroyer of the gods" (as Larry Hurtado puts it in his recent book),[32] in the same ways as Luke observed this happening in first century Antioch.

Persecution helps the church to grow. The gospel broke boundaries of class and ethnicity. The church triumphed because the Lord's hand was with them, as they preached the unerring word of God and refuted error. Key individuals played a part, but the way the early Christians applied their faith in love and good deeds was crucial in their success, as was excluding those who did not teach the saving truth of the gospel.

This is how the church grew and multiplied in the first few decades and centuries. It is probably how the church will survive and grow and flourish for the next few centuries too, until the Lord of the church himself returns to gather us from east and west and north and south, and usher in his new creation.

May our Lord Jesus Christ himself and God our Father, who loved us and by his grace gave us eternal encouragement and good hope, encourage our hearts and strengthen us in every good deed and word. And may the message of the Lord spread rapidly and be honoured—just as it was in the first three centuries. Please deliver us from wicked and evil people, for not everyone has faith. But help us trust in your faithfulness to strengthen and protect us from the evil one, as we continue to do the things that you command us in your word. Direct our hearts into God's love and Christ's perseverance in the power of your Spirit. Amen.

Lee Gatiss *is the Director of Church Society and Lecturer in Church History at Union School of Theology.*

32 Larry W. Hurtado, *Destroyer of the Gods: Early Christian Distinctiveness in the Roman World* (Waco, TX.: Baylor University Press, 2016).

POSITIVELY ANGLICAN

Building on the foundations and transforming the church

"Challenges the status quo with biblical theology, historical narrative, and practical application regarding the modern Church in England (and around the world)."

Foley Beach

Archbishop and Primate, Anglican Church in North America

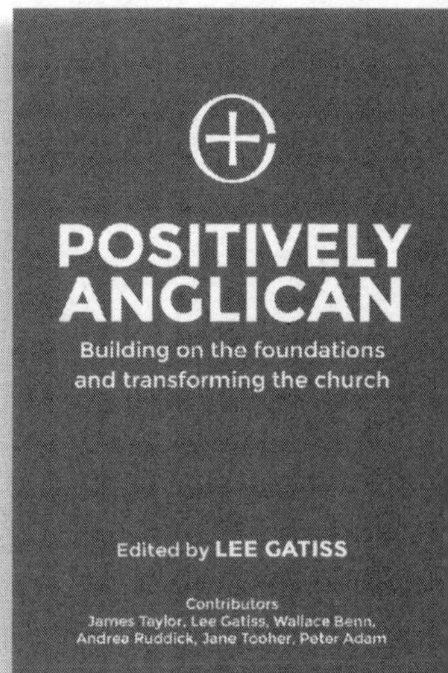

With the church in the state it's in, how can evangelicals be more positive and enthusiastic about being Anglican? Is it worth sticking with it, when we face hostility both from our surrounding culture and from within the church itself?

The authors of this book reimagine an energetically optimistic Anglican future, and renew our confidence in the transforming power of God's word. They provide a compelling vision of an uncompromising and entrepreneurial evangelicalism, true to its theological roots while engaging the wider church with integrity and consistency.

"A valuable contribution to how 'mutual flourishing' can work out from a conservative evangelical perspective."

Paul Butler, *Bishop of Durham*

"Celebrates the fact that our being Anglican is not born of pragmatism, but of theological conviction."

Mike Cain, *Emmanuel Church, Bristol*

UK orders to Church Society:
www.churchsociety.org
admin@churchsociety.org or call 01923 255410.
Published by Lost Coin Books for Church Society
ISBN: 9781784981020

LOST COIN

Church Society